THE UNLIKELY HERO

Heinrich Schliemann's Quest for Troy

Illustrated by
Grisha Dotzenko

Whittlesey House

McGraw-Hill Book Company, Inc. New York Toronto London

THE
UNLIKELY
HERO

Heinrich Schliemann's quest for Troy

by
ALAN HONOUR

Also by Alan Honour

CAVE OF RICHES: The ory of the Dead Sea Scrolls

TEN MILES HIGH, TWO M ES DEEP: The Adventures of the Piccards

For my parents

Against This Background

THE NINETEENTH CENTURY was a smug century.

In 1822, Queen Victoria was three years old. She seemed remote from the throne of England and the astonishing era to which she was to give her name, as remote, indeed, as was Heinrich Schliemann from the vast fortune and fame that were to be his.

As time passed, Queen Victoria grew into her destined role—a living symbol and proof indeed that "God's in His heaven / All's right with the world!" Kings, lords, nobles and peasants—each knew his place in the scheme of things; each kept his place.

America, too, was smug. There, people decided that progress had been so rapid that everything man could invent had been invented. They talked seriously of abolishing the patent office. Since there was nothing left to invent, what sense to keep a useless patent office open?

In truth, progress had been made in many dazzling ways. But the smug possessors of the nineteenth century little realized they were astride a volcano of progress. Many of them lived to see this volcano erupt, bemoaning the loss of their happy days and peaceful lives, the end of the selfish world they had helped to create.

Jules Verne would soon be writing *Twenty Thousand Leagues Under the Sea, Around the World in Eighty*

7

Days, and other science fiction stories—a sure sign of what was coming. These yarns were all best sellers. But, of course, nobody in his right mind seriously believed in submarines or aircraft. They were pretty fancies at best, but quite impossible!

This was the world into which Heinrich Schliemann was born. Heinrich Schliemann's life, as it unfolded, followed remarkably and dramatically the pattern of the world about him.

This strange human being, Heinrich Schliemann, whose spirit was tormented so many years of his life by conflicting values, made important contributions to the progress of mankind in ways quite different. His business enterprises in America and Europe played a significant part in helping to bring into being the great industrial expansion then beginning. His journeys into man's past —to the supposedly mythical cities of Troy, Mycenae, and others—established the factual truth of the existence of these cities and the heroes who built and lived in them. Whole civilizations previously thought to be the creation of an imaginative poet, Homer, were proved by Schliemann to be real.

Heinrich Schliemann pointed the way that led to understanding and truth, where before there had been only mystery, doubt, skepticism, and conjecture.

In all these tasks, Heinrich Schliemann served his fellow men well.

Contents

CHAPTER 1

Grocery Boy

JANUARY 6, 1822, was bitterly cold, as winter days can be in the old German duchy of Mecklenburg, bordering Poland and the Baltic Sea.

Heavy snow covered the ground and piled in odd shapes on the rooftops. There was no motor traffic to break the quiet. Only the wind roared in the streets, interrupted now and then by the clanking of bells of a horse-drawn sleigh or cart. Laughter and warmth skittered about in the cold air as villagers left taverns or opened shop doors. People hurried about their business, anxious to get back to the comfort of their own firesides.

The child who entered life that cold winter day in the tiny town of Neu Buckow, Heinrich Schliemann, was to know coldness in many forms most of his life.

But at first, he was warm and well cared for.

When Heinrich was two years old, the family moved to the small village of Ankershagen. In this village, even tinier than the place of his birth, Heinrich spent the next nine years.

Pastor Schliemann, Heinrich's father, was as big, bluff,

11

and hearty as the people whose religious needs he served
—some of the time. His community was smug, well content with its way of life. But the pastor was very poor
and had four daughters and a son to feed as well as Heinrich. The man grew increasingly frustrated as time
passed, for he fared no better in Ankershagen than he
had at Neu Buckow. When the ache of poverty hurt him
most, Pastor Schliemann was very bitter and cruel. At
such times he made life miserable for Frau Schliemann,
his wife, and his six children.

Heinrich hated these dark days of coldness. Heinrich and his brother Ludwig, although usually they were
not close, did their best to keep out of the pastor's way
when he was in bad moods. Hardly a word would be
spoken in the house. When the home was gloomy, Heinrich would try to hide in the warmth of his mother's
arms. He was bewildered by the frequent, sudden
changes of his father's moods.

"Mamma," the boy asked one day, "why does Papa get
into such a rage?"

Frau Schliemann looked wistfully down at the thin,
pale, lank-haired child clinging to her knees. She took
the pinched face between her hands. "Poverty does
strange things to people, Heinrich," she said. "Some
people manage to rise above it. Others sink beneath its
deadening burden."

She seemed to forget that the small boy could not be
expected to understand what she was talking about. She
rose from her chair and went to the steaming pot on the
stove.

But these times of gloom were temporary. When the pastor was in a good mood, he seemed only too anxious to make up for the trouble he caused. Then Heinrich would forget his bewilderment and be happy—until the next time.

Pastor Schliemann and his wife both had some learning. Fortunately for Heinrich, the pastor respected knowledge and taught his children to read and write as soon as they were able.

The best times of all were when the pastor agreed to tell stories. Heinrich was more eager than the rest and as soon as he spotted his father in good temper he ran to him.

"Papa," he cried, "tell us a story please. Please, Papa!"

"What would you like to hear, young man?"

"Oh, Papa, tell us about the robber baron!"

Pastor Schliemann began the legend of the ruined castle which lay just beyond the village.

"Once the castle was proud and strong. From the castle, Baron Hennig von Holstein carried terror to all the villages round about. One day, the Duke of Mecklenburg set out to put an end to von Holstein's raiding. But the robber baron learned of the duke's plan and set an ambush. A cowherd saw what the baron was doing and ran off to warn the duke. When Baron von Holstein heard this, he was furious. He set a trap and captured the poor cowherd. He carried him off to the castle and roasted him on a spit. Then he kicked the body for good measure, he was so angry. But the duke still came after him, and, seeing that he would lose the battle, the baron hastily buried all his treasure near the tower in the castle, and then killed himself.

"The cowherd and the baron were buried in the castle graveyard," Heinrich's father went on, "and 'tis said, on certain days, the foot that kicked the roasted cowherd can be seen, clad in a black stocking, poking up from the grave and waving about in the air!"

Always, at the end of the spine-tingling story, Heinrich said, "Papa, if we're so poor, why don't we go and dig up the baron's treasure?"

Pastor Schliemann smiled, then sent Heinrich and his brother and sisters packing off to bed. And Heinrich always lay awake, dreaming of digging up the treasure. He was certain it was there, somewhere!

Many times Heinrich went out to the old castle, where he sat for hours waiting patiently for the black-stockinged leg to appear. He never saw it. But he still believed.

From the time he was a small boy, Heinrich fed his soul on tales of buried treasure. He loved to hear the stories of the brooding, lake-riven countryside around Ankershagen. He believed each ghost-ridden tale, each legend of the Teuton and Slav people locked in battle for possession of the North German plains. He always came back to the story of the robber baron's buried treasure. He simply could not understand why his father did not search for it.

"I have told you many times, Heinrich, it is just a story. Perhaps it happened, but I would be laughed at if I went poking about the graveyard looking for buried treasure."

Heinrich was not convinced.

Heinrich was overjoyed, at the age of seven, when his father gave him a copy of Jerrer's *Illustrated History of the World*. He delighted in the big book so full of graphic pictures.

He read every word of the book, but one story above all captured him and held his interest. That was the story of the siege of Troy. Accompanying it was a wonderful picture showing the burning of Troy. For the next three years, Heinrich was seldom far away from his beloved history book. At every opportunity he pestered his father to talk with him about Troy.

At first, Pastor Schliemann encouraged his son in this interest. Then, as time passed and the troubled man grew more surly, he laughed at Heinrich and told him not to be ridiculous. "Why, boy, most people don't even believe Troy ever existed! They say the whole tale is only an invention of the blind poet Homer. Some say even Homer didn't exist!"

"But Papa, look at those huge stones in the picture! Fire and burning could not destroy those. The man who drew this picture believed Homer. He has described Troy exactly as the book does. *I believe in Homer, too!* Some day, Papa, I shall find Troy and dig it out of the ground. All the treasure will be mine. But I shall look after you, Papa, and you will not be poor again."

The pastor rejected Heinrich's childish offer and the love that went with it. "You are stupid, boy," he said angrily. "There is no such place as Troy."

Nursing his hurt and hiding his tears, Heinrich turned

again to the stories of the *Iliad* and the *Odyssey*. They
became more real to him than ever, and he nourished his
imagination and lavished his love on the long-dead heroes
of the past. He believed in their reality with all his
heart.

His favorite part of the stories centered on the fall of
Troy. Over and over, Heinrich read of Troy until he
knew the story by heart:

King Priam had sent his son Prince Paris on a mission

"Some day, I shall find Troy."

to the semibarbaric Achaean kings.   Paris had seen the wife of King Menelaus, the beautiful Helen.   He fell in love with her and carried her off to Troy.

Furious at this affront, Menelaus summoned the kings together.   Helen's was the lovely "face that launched a thousand ships."   Sailing to the stronghold of Priam, the Achaeans laid siege to Troy.   Troy withstood them gallantly.   But besides vengeance for Helen, the Achaeans wanted to seize the incredible treasure of Troy.

Hector was killed by Achilles in a duel.

They did not know that much of the vast treasure had been buried, within the city, as a precautionary measure against defeat.

In the ensuing battles and duels, Hector, Priam's son, was killed by Achilles in a personal duel. The terrible brutality wreaked upon the dead body of Hector caused renewed fighting. Achilles was slain by Paris, who shot an arrow into his heel, the only vulnerable spot on the strong man's body.

Tiring of the long siege after these events, the Achaeans resorted to trickery. They made a show of defeat and sailed away. They left an immense wooden horse before the gates of Troy. Thinking this a tribute, the Trojans dragged the horse into their city. Priam's daughter, Cassandra, warned them of trouble, but since she had always been thought slightly mad, nobody paid any attention.

A night of merrymaking and celebration of victory followed. Still refusing to heed Cassandra, the exhausted Trojans slept, leaving the walls unguarded.

Quietly, the Achaean ships sailed back to shore. They had hidden soldiers in the wooden horse and these men now emerged from the belly of the horse and opened the gates of Troy. The merciless Achaeans slaughtered and burned with shocking savagery. When they were done, Troy had vanished in a pile of smoking ruins—gone, the proud, crowded, and beautiful city. Nothing remained.

Whenever he could, Heinrich persuaded his few playmates to go to the castle ruins and act out the heroic deeds of the Trojans. Soon, however, they got bored with his love of the Trojan story. They turned to laughter and mockery of Heinrich's fantastic games.

Heinrich withdrew more and more into a shell of loneliness and solitude.

When he was eleven years old, the icy fingers of coldness once more reached out for Heinrich's heart. Frau Schliemann died, leaving her family with nobody who knew how to handle the pastor and keep her children together. Abruptly, Heinrich's world was smashed.

After his wife died, the pastor seemed to lose all sense of control. His parishioners became angry with him. They stopped going to church. Suddenly, there was no money. The only thing to do was break up the family.

Sad and bewildered by these rapid events, Heinrich was packed off to live with his uncle Friedrich at Kalkhorst, also in Mecklenburg.

For all his hurt, the hard cold lump of grief in his heart, Heinrich knew he had to get on with the business of living. Right now, this meant school. He was eager to begin.

Uncle Friedrich was not a rich man, as he explained to Heinrich. "You are old enough to understand things now, boy. Your father has sent little enough money to send you to school. There are no free schools, you understand. But we will do our best for you, eh?"

Uncle Friedrich enrolled the young lad, thrust unwillingly on his care, in the *Gymnasium* at Neustrelitz. This was more advanced than an elementary school, more like a preparatory school. He was delighted that Heinrich soon proved himself well above average in his ability to learn. Heinrich mastered Latin, writing and reading it with growing skill. But outside his studies, he was a very unhappy boy. He could not shake the feeling of being unwanted. He had little appetite and developed into a gaunt, haggard, ugly youth. But his soul fed on his books and studies and his eyes were bright and dark in the pale face.

A driving ambition began to possess the lonely boy. He studied hard, hoping to enter the University of Rostock. The university dated from 1419 and Rostock was an important commercial center. The opportunities he hoped to find there drew Heinrich on.

Then, the icy fingers of cold tightened further their grip upon Heinrich Schliemann. His father had so outraged his congregation with behavior unbecoming to a pastor that he was censured by his bishop and suspended from the ministry until he mended his ways.

"I am sorry, Heinrich," Uncle Friedrich said, when he reported the matter. "I cannot afford to pay for your schooling. The best I can do for you is send you to the *Realschule* (elementary). Perhaps your father will send enough money to pay the small fees there."

So Heinrich attended an elementary school. His cleverness carried him many classes ahead of those normal for a boy his age, and when he was fourteen, in 1836, he had advanced to the top class.

Then fell the disastrous blow that ended once and for all his hope of an education.

"You will have to find a job, Heinrich," his uncle told him one day. "Your father refuses to send even the pittance needed to keep you at the *Realschule*. He says he can't afford it. Times are hard, boy, and I cannot afford to pay your fees."

"But Uncle, what am I to do?" Heinrich wailed, tears running down his face. "I *must* have an education!"

"I am sorry for you, Heinrich, but I can do no more. It might be best if you returned to Ankershagen, although heaven knows what you will find there."

Heinrich lay awake that night trying to solve his problems. For a while, he was terrified of what lay ahead. Loneliness, insecurity, and rejection had killed whatever humor Heinrich had. But it also forced him to adopt grim self-reliance.

Ambition came to his rescue. The force of his will would not let him go down in defeat. He put aside his dream of the university. Where could a poor boy ever find the money to attend such a school? There was but one thing to do: work! He *had* to work to keep body and soul together. He had no desire to return to Ankershagen and be mocked by acquaintances for his poverty and his father's strange behavior.

Heinrich wrapped his few belongings, which now included cheap copies of Homer's *Iliad* and *Odyssey,* into a small bundle. There was no work to be found in Neustrelitz; so, with dragging feet he trudged from village to village.

At Fürstenberg, he finally found a job. He became a grocery boy at the shop of Herr Holtz. The pay was very small, a few pence a week. But at least he had access to food and he was allowed to sleep under the counter. He made his bed beneath the counter and kept his few books tucked away in his blanket.

When he felt like it, Heinrich nibbled on a piece of sausage or chewed black bread, but he had little appetite for food. He grew more gaunt-looking than ever. Rising at dawn, he swept the shop, cleaned the counters, and lugged boxes and barrels of herrings and potatoes from the storage room into the shop. Late at night, exhausted, he stumbled onto his hard bed, barely able to keep his eyes open long enough to browse for a few minutes in his Homer.

The more willing Heinrich was to please, the more was demanded of him. He swept, dusted, and carried heavy packages until he was ready to drop. He soon developed a racking cough that prevented him from sleeping well. A cold hatred of his servility took hold of him. Every hour of every day his hatred of poverty grew until he was obsessed by a desire never again to be in such a position.

Only one bright spot colored his slaving at the grocery. A young wastrel, a few years older than Heinrich, began to visit the shop for an occasional glass of potato wine. He had some education, and, like Heinrich, had fallen on evil days. Heinrich was delighted to discover that this young man could read over a hundred lines of Homer in the original Greek. Whenever he could, he passed a glass of potato schnapps to the young man in exchange for hearing him recite Homer aloud. Heinrich was captivated by the beauty of the language, although he didn't understand a word.

He was horrified, one day, to discover his mind and

body so tired and overworked that all memory of what he had learned at school had deserted him.

"I have tried," he said to his young acquaintance, "but I remember nothing!   What am I to do?"

"You should get out of this shop, Heinrich.   That cough will not improve while you stay here.   Go to the city.   Try something else.   I shall miss you and the glasses of wine, but you ought to leave here."

All Heinrich could see, with pangs of envy in his heart, was other boys his age, going and coming from school. They were gay and happy, well fed and cared for.   His own state was a poor comparison.

Cold resolution seized him.   "I will go," he said, handing his friend a glass of wine.   "Somehow, I will grow rich.   I will educate myself.   I will make them take notice of me and honor me as a scholar should be honored!"

It was a lofty ambition, easy to dream, hard to make real.   He had little money.   His old patched suit hardly helped his appearance.   He knew nothing except handling groceries.   But his resolution held.

"Herr Holtz," he said, when his mind was made up. "You can find somebody else to slave with your sausage and potatoes.   I am leaving at once!"

Dumfounded, Herr Holtz stared as Heinrich gathered his bundle and walked out of the shop.

Heinrich set out for the big seaport at Hamburg.   As he trudged the long road to the city, he dreamed of a better future.   He might be lucky enough, in Hamburg, to get on a ship and make his way to America.   There, he had heard, the streets were paved with gold!

CHAPTER 2

The Unhappy Sailor

HEINRICH SCHLIEMANN arrived in the North Sea port of Hamburg, dusty, weary, and hungry beyond belief. He was very weak. His sore feet ached badly. Only his great determination had enabled him to get this far without dropping in despair.

But as he trudged along the cobbled streets, drawing nearer to the heart of Hamburg, his spirits rose. He was awestruck by the noise, the sounds all about. He forgot his hunger and misery for a while. Surely here he would find work.

Heinrich was used only to small towns and villages. He had never before seen so many people clustered in one place. The busy port was vast, and for hours he wandered the streets, munching a hunk of bread. He was dazed by the different activities the city showed him.

He found a secondhand bookstall in a market place. Leafing through the books and papers, he chanced upon an old book containing the elements of bookkeeping. For a few pence, he bought the book. Nursing his small sum of money, he took the cheapest lodging he could find,

24

then settled down to find a job. When he was not hunt-
ing work, he studied bookkeeping. Rapidly, he learned
by heart all that was in the book. He hoped this would
help him get a better job than in the grocery shop at
Fürstenberg.

Lacking an appetite, it was easy for him to deny himself food. The bony, emaciated figure looked more like
a scarecrow than the heroic Greeks he worshiped. But
their stories continued to feed his soul, enrich his spirit,
and the dark eyes still burned feverishly above the sallow
cheeks.

Heinrich did his best and eventually he found a job.
His employer set him to work making entries in huge
ledgers. The bookkeeping proved useful and Heinrich
found the figures fascinating. He worked well and hard.
But the stuffy atmosphere of the office irritated his chest.
The wheezing cough started to be troublesome again.
He began the habit of wandering down near the water's
edge to take cold baths in quiet unpeopled spots. Each
morning he plunged into the cold sea. This, he hoped,
would toughen him up and stop the cough.

But his employer took a sudden dislike to the ugly,
pale-faced young man who was always wheezing about the
office. Without bothering to give Heinrich reasons, he
fired the new apprentice.

Once again, Heinrich was on the streets and almost
penniless. He took to wandering about the immense
docksides hoping and longing to find a ship bound for
America. The hard shell of his lonely isolation thick-
ened about him. Cold baths were no substitute for good,

nourishing food, or warm human love and companionship. Humorless and sour-faced though he was, his ambition pushed him on. It was the only real thing he had
and he clung to it fast.

Then luck took pity on him. One day, while roaming
the docks, watching the ships loading and unloading,
Heinrich saw a man he knew. The youth stared, then
ran after the man.

"Herr Wendt," he called panting. He forced the un-
used muscles of his face into a sort of smile, more like a
grimace. "Don't you know me, Herr Wendt?" The
puzzled man looked at Heinrich. "I am Frau Schliemann's son."

"Ah, yes," Herr Wendt replied. "And how is your
dear mother?"

"She is dead many years," Heinrich answered.

"I am sorry to hear that," said Herr Wendt. "What
brings you to Hamburg?"

Heinrich hesitated, not knowing where to begin.

Herr Wendt studied the peculiar-looking young fellow
confronting him. "Come," he said abruptly. "I am going to eat lunch. You look as if you could use a good
heavy meal."

It was a fortunate meeting for Heinrich. Over a plate
of the first warm food he'd had in a long time, he poured
out his sufferings to Herr Wendt. He talked of his hope
of shipping off to America.

"I don't know, Heinrich," Herr Wendt said. "My
business handles a good deal of shipping, but you know
nothing of ships or the sea. Still, for the sake of your

mother, I will see what I can do.   I am meeting a ship's captain in two days.   Come to me then and we shall see if there is a chance for you.   Here," he said, handing Heinrich his address and a small sum of money.   "This will help you until then."

Heinrich rose from the table and thanked Herr Wendt gratefully.   "I shall be there."

Gazing after the strange young lad, Herr Wendt pitied him.   "Such troubles for such young shoulders," he sighed.   "Surely," he thought, "that young lad is far worse off than Oliver Twist, the boy I just finished reading about in that new book by Charles Dickens!"   Yet he found himself admiring the lad's courage.   "How many," he mused, "would have faced up to the tragedy which has troubled that lad's steps?"

Heinrich's good luck held.   Herr Wendt introduced him to the captain of the brig *Dorothea*.   The square-rigged, two-masted sailing vessel was soon to leave on a voyage to Venezuela.

Heinrich could hardly credit his good luck.   After a brief conversation with the captain, he was signed on as a cabin boy.   The captain warned him of the rigors of life at sea, but Heinrich did not fear them.   Anything was better than his present condition.   It meant nothing to Heinrich, nor apparently to the captain, that Heinrich knew nothing about ships or the sea.   Herr Wendt vouched for the lad, and the boy seemed willing enough, even though he looked as if a strong puff of wind would bowl him off his feet.

Heinrich used most of the little money he had left to

purchase a change of clothes, at second hand. Then he bought an old Spanish grammar. He reasoned, it is a Spanish-speaking part of the world to which I'm bound, therefore I will take advantage of the time ahead at sea to learn the language. This was the first step in the new and better life he had promised himself.

Feeling almost gay, Heinrich clambered up the gangway and reported to the mate.

Pointing to the forward deck the mate said, "Stow your gear in the crew's quarters down below. Then hustle back on deck and lend a hand casting off."

The smell of tar, salt air, wet rope, and paint exhilarated Heinrich. He quickly found his quarters, picked a corner, then hurried back on deck. It was very cold and winter was fast approaching. Heinrich shivered, but cheered up at the thought he would soon be in the warm tropic waters off South America. He bustled about with the rest of the sailors, stowing ropes, battening hatches, helping wherever he was summoned. The hectic activity pleased him. "Cast off, Mr. Mate," the captain called. "Cast off," the mate yelled to the sailors on the mooring lines. Heinrich watched, glad to be leaving the misery of the past behind.

On November 28, 1841, the *Dorothea* sailed from Hamburg, and with a heady breeze slowly made her way down the river Elbe to Helgoland Bay and the North Sea.

From the moment the ship eased away from the side of her berth, Heinrich was seasick. He was in a very bad way when the ship called briefly at Cuxhaven. He considered, for a moment, leaving the ship. But his courage did not desert him. He stayed aboard.

A sailor told him, "If you keep munching hardtack biscuits, and there's plenty aboard this ship, the stuff will swell in your stomach and ease the pain. Then, when you have to be sick, you'll have something to get rid of."

Heinrich followed this advice, but it did not help much.

Out of Cuxhaven, the *Dorothea* ran into heavy weather. Heinrich was too ill to move about much or be of any help on deck. The half-humorous taunts of the crew did not make him feel better. He kept to his bunk and suffered the retching pains in silence. He clamped his teeth tight behind his thin lips and tried to lose himself in learning Spanish.

He studied every word in the book, and its meaning, repeating each one over and over to practice pronunciation. The rolling, creaking ship seemed to set a rhythm that followed the words.

A few days later, off the coast of Holland, the ship was struck by tempest weather. Members of the crew began to mutter of a curse on the voyage. Superstitious sailors cast baleful glances at Heinrich, huddled on his bunk, muttering Spanish words to the air. He paid them as little heed as possible.

Almost immediately, the ship started to take on water. The pumps had to be kept going night and day. Heinrich struggled on deck, taking his turn with the rest at the pumps. His head felt three times its normal size.

For a while, the captain held his own against the buf-

feting winds and torrents of rain, keeping on course.
Then, the wind worsened. The rain turned to snow and
icy sleet. Wisps of fog drifted around the *Dorothea*. The
ship's timbers began to rattle and creak ominously.

Sick, and tired from his turn at the pumps, Heinrich
stumbled to his bunk. He did not hear the mate yell,
"Stay awake, we might have to abandon ship if things get
worst!"

The stuffy atmosphere of the cabin after the tearing
winds on deck made Heinrich's stomach retch. He
stripped off his clothes and lay down on his bunk. He
was so ill he passed beyond the fear and panic now at-
tacking the crew. He was too exhausted to know what
was going on, or care. He dozed in fitful sleep.

A huge green-black wave struck the ship head on.
When the tons of salt water, glittering with phosphorus,
washed overboard again, they took the ship's mast with
them. The crippled ship was drifting out of control, and
the captain tried to drop anchor. But the great iron
chains snapped like rotted rope.

Frightened cries of "Abandon ship!" brought Heinrich back to life. A seaman dashed into the cabin, "Everyone on deck!" he ordered. "Man the boats!"

Not thinking of his condition, Heinrich struggled to the
deck. The lifeboats were smashed, one after another,
as the crew tried to lower them into the mountainous
seas. It was very dark, bitterly cold, and snow and sleet
still fell like sharp needles.

Heinrich, struggling to pierce the gloom, clung to the
rigging, naked as the day he was born. He forgot his

nakedness, forgot the cold, forgot the bitter wind that was trying to tear his grip away from the ropes. He clung on. Desperately he prayed to God for safety. The sea slapped the ship around as if she were no more than a matchstick.

The *Dorothea* gave a sudden lurch, then turned over. She was completely gone in a matter of seconds.

Screaming with fear, Heinrich was flung far over the side into the murky, bitterly cold sea. He rose to the surface, amazed to find his mind was calm and working properly. "I must have imagined screaming," he thought, embarrassed. A barrel floated by, and he clutched it frantically. It rested him and kept him afloat.

Numbed with cold, his hands fixed to the barrel in a grip of death, he drifted with the sea, slowly passing into the welcome warmth of unconsciousness. Heinrich was only dimly aware of the hands that reached down from a boat and pulled him aboard.

"Poor soul," a voice muttered as Heinrich tumbled down in the bottom of the boat, snuggling for warmth to the other survivors snuggled there. He was cut and bruised. Every part of his body ached.

For hours, the small boat with fourteen survivors aboard drifted with the cold dark sea. It had miraculously floated free when the ship capsized. But all the oars had gone, and the survivors could do nothing but drift.

A cold, gray dawn painted a somber line across the horizon. Along with cargo and wreckage of the late *Dorothea*, the small boat was drifting toward an island shore in the distance. When the gray line reached halfway

Heinrich was flung into the cold sea.

across the sky, the boat beached itself. The exhausted survivors lay where they were, unable to shift. All around, people of the island rushed to the beach to collect shares of the loot the troubled sea had presented to them. They did not see, or else ignored, the small boat in their midst.

"Look!" cried one man, dragging a large bale of woolen cloth out of the water. "This should bring me a pretty penny!" He laughed with glee. Another answered, dragging a broken box of cheeses up the beach: "This, too, will sell very nicely."

Then a farmer drove up in his cart and took the shivering survivors to his nearby farmhouse. "Do not mind the villagers," the farmer said. "Folks here are very poor and these are hard times. They will make good use of the 'gifts' from the sea for many a month to come."

For several days the survivors stayed at the farmhouse, gathering their strength. They had washed ashore on the island of Texel, one of the Frisian Islands, just off the coast of Holland.

"Here," said the farmer to Heinrich, "put these on and cover your nakedness. You are ugly, boy."

Heinrich noticed that he smiled, however, and took the clothes and the pair of clogs that didn't fit.

Then, wonder of wonders, Heinrich's seabox floated ashore and was brought to the farmhouse. His belongings, books, and introductions from Herr Wendt to Venezuela, were dry and safe. He could not know it, of course, but this was the first of many occasions when the sea would treat him badly, then nourish him, following bad fortune with good.

The feeling of relief at his amazing rescue quieted down. What should he do now? he wondered. He had no prospects and little hope. The world was, indeed, a bitter and cold place.

The rescued crewmen decided to make their way back to Hamburg.

"I shall not go back to that hulking great city," Heinrich said. He had known precious little to be pleased with there. He stayed on with the farmer a few days more, then decided to try his fortune in Holland, since God had chosen to set him down there.

With determination, the youth set out for the city of Amsterdam.

CHAPTER 3

How to Become a Millionaire

"BETTER THAN FIVE YEARS have passed," Heinrich mused, as he walked the road to Amsterdam. "What is there to show for my efforts since I left Herr Holtz's shop at Fürstenberg?"

Grimly, he strode on. Thinking of Fürstenberg made him think of Mecklenburg. In Amsterdam, Mecklenburg had a consulate, and Heinrich decided to make his way there as soon as he reached the city. "After all," he thought, "they're supposed to help stranded people from Mecklenburg, so they must help me!"

Boldly, Heinrich knocked on the door of the consulate. A servant answered. The man was so shocked by Heinrich's unkempt, ragged appearance that he refused even to speak to him. He slammed the door in Heinrich's face.

Heinrich had determination, if nothing else, so he tried again. This time, he managed to get his troubles to the ear of the consul. But the consul could hardly be bothered. He gave his servant a few cents for Heinrich, barely enough for a decent meal.

Far from being crushed by these experiences, Heinrich's resolve to succeed grew stronger. It seemed to him that, in the hard world he knew, respect and sympathy were things to be bought. Very well then, he would become rich enough to buy them! He loathed poverty, raggedness, and the humiliation of seeking aid from others who begrudged what little they ever gave.

Heinrich spoke not a word of Dutch, and this fact set him more remote from the life around him than ever. The Dutch, he saw, were jolly and prosperous. Well, he too would be prosperous.

Coldly, ruthlessly, he made his plans. Heinrich found a shabby room in a sailors' lodgings, promising to pay as soon as money reached him from home. Since he had no home and only one friend, he had to use that friend. He wrote at once to Herr Wendt, telling him all that had happened and the fate of the *Dorothea*. He explained his situation and begged a small loan.

Heinrich was lucky. Not only did Herr Wendt send him a princely sum equivalent to about sixty dollars, he enclosed a letter of introduction to the Prussian consulate, asking that they assist Heinrich wherever possible.

Heinrich vowed he would justify this beginning and that upon this basis he would build his fortune. He purchased a suit of decent clothes and presented himself to the Prussian consul with Herr Wendt's letter.

"I do not seek charity," Heinrich said proudly, almost arrogantly. "I know bookkeeping very well and I wish to find work in a countinghouse."

The consul, himself full of arrogance, liked Heinrich's

attitude. He noted down details and promised to see what he could do.

Very soon, Heinrich was sent for, and found himself the possessor of a job. He was employed as messenger. He was pleased. At last he had a foot in the door of the business world. He handled large sums of money, carrying bills of exchange back and forth between his employer and the banks. He liked the feel of good solid money, even though it was not his own. "This is the world," thought Heinrich, "where fortunes are made!"

Heinrich nursed his salary and what was left of the money Herr Wendt sent him. He denied himself all luxury, even some necessities. No sacrifice was too severe, too demanding. For entertainment, he walked in the streets, pressing his face close to the windows of elegant shops to admire the treasures behind the glass. Calculatingly, he set about climbing to the top of the world of business.

Studying the habits and faces of the men he met in his work, Heinrich soon noted that the business world of his time was a jungle. The strong and ruthless survived —the weak went to the wall. Heinrich vowed he would survive. He set himself the task of acquiring the tools that would lead him to success.

Amsterdam was a large commercial city. Much of its wealth came from the immense import-export business it handled. It was a great clearing house for goods from all parts of the world. How best to conquer this world?

Encouragement came from his employer. Finding Heinrich honest and willing, almost fanatically devoted to the business, his employer increased the young man's salary, and his responsibilities. This gratified Heinrich. Grimly he plunged on. He had no time for girls, no time to make friends. Every spare waking moment, he worked.

Import-export, he realized, needed men with a command of languages. If he had languages at his command, many doors would open to him. So, reluctantly, Heinrich put aside his books of Greek heroic figures. He purchased Dutch, German, and English dictionaries. His Mecklenburg speech was a German dialect which helped his choice for a beginning. He bought cheap copy books and made long lists of words, repeating the procedure he had found useful with his Spanish grammar. Whenever he came across a person who spoke good Dutch or German, he engaged himself in conversation with that person as long as he dared, talking business affairs. In a very few months, he mastered Dutch and German. What gaps there were in his knowledge, he knew, would quickly fill with practice and experience. He could read and write both tongues passably well and he improved steadily.

English he found a little harder, but he persisted. Time passed. Loneliness he did not notice. He was engrossed in his studies.

Heinrich began to go to the English church in Amsterdam. He listened carefully to the sermons with all the concentration he could command. He learned a great deal about the little island across the sea, now growing ever more powerful. He stood listening to the conversation of the English people after church, copying their

speech parrot fashion. Whenever he could, he singled one
out and tried to speak the language.

Some looked with superior amusement at the ugly
young man who spoke so earnestly with such an atrocious
accent. Heinrich did not notice. All he cared about
was their manner of speaking. Many of the words he
could speak he did not understand, but it did not matter.
The gist of his conversation was always understood.
Fluency, again, would come with time and practice. He
wrote essays in the strange tongue, and made faithful
copics of the sermons, which were sometimes printed
and handed to the congregation.

Diligence and concentration brought rewards. Heinrich discovered that the more he concentrated, the easier
learning became. His powers developed rapidly and he
found that some rules of grammar held true in nearly all
languages. Each tongue he tackled became easier to
master than the previous one.

It was not long before Heinrich had at his command a
good working knowledge of most of the languages important to success in the import-export business. English was
followed by Italian and French, and he brushed up his
Spanish and added Portuguese. Now, he believed, he had
something to offer that would be extremely valuable.

Necessity had been a good teacher. At twenty-two,
Heinrich was ready to pursue the next phase of his plan
to conquer the business world. He did not worry that he
had no degrees to offer. He had a working knowledge of
many languages that would have taken years and years

to acquire at school. All he had to do was show he could read and write seven languages. Surely *somebody* would give him a chance to show what he could do.

Heinrich hunted in Amsterdam for a likely business where he might put his newly acquired knowledge to work. He chose the biggest import-export house in the city. In the spring of 1844, he had an interview with Herr Schröder, head of the firm.

Bemusedly, Herr Schröder listened to the strange young man with the piercing dark eyes explain his special qualifications. He rather doubted Heinrich had taught himself the languages he spoke in so short a time. But he didn't think that really mattered. He considered himself a good judge of character, and this earnest fellow might prove useful to the firm. He was also well aware of the uses to which Heinrich's languages could be put.

"Very well," he said, when Heinrich finished. "I will give you a trial. You will do some bookkeeping and answer some of our foreign correspondence. You may start work tomorrow."

Feeling intensely pleased with himself, Heinrich thanked his new employer and withdrew. The salary Herr Schröder said he would pay amounted to the equivalent of $150 a month! It was a tremendous sum to Heinrich. His self-confidence soared.

The change of status did not affect Heinrich's habits. He was still like a miser hoarding his pennies. He bought more language books and read everything he could lay his hands on about imports and exports. He spent all of his spare time studying ship's cargoes and attending the auction rooms where cargoes were sold. He noted how a man who could speak quickly in the tongue of the buyer or seller could often turn a quick profit while others depended upon tiresome translations. He obtained many lucrative cargoes for Schröder's because of his ability and quick mind.

For his pleasure and relaxation, he still took long walks, staring into shop windows full of luxuries, and continued his cold baths. It was a truly Spartan régimen, and a price would be demanded. But Heinrich was unaware of this.

Herr Schröder was well pleased with Heinrich Schliemann. It gratified his vanity that once again he had picked a smart man. He summoned Heinrich to his office one day.

"Herr Schliemann," he said pleasantly, "I am well pleased with you. Henceforth, you are to be our chief correspondent. Your salary will be doubled. How does that suit you, eh?"

Heinrich was satisfied. He had proved his point. But he did not relax; this success merely sharpened his determination.

"Thank you, Herr Schröder," he said. "I shall continue to try and give you my best services."

Already Heinrich had dipped into his savings to make small investments. Often he bought small quantities of indigo, then quickly resold it before other buyers noticed that the deal had been closed. Gleefully, he counted his pennies and watched his hoarded savings grow rapidly.

Indigo, he decided, held promise of great profit. The

indigo plant was imported from India, where it grew, in immense quantities. From Amsterdam and other centers, it was resold and shipped all over the world to be crushed and pressed for the blue dye. Gradually, Heinrich increased his private purchasing of portions of cargoes, selling them at once to other buyers. And his savings multiplied.

Heinrich had yet to realize that his determination to succeed in the business world was taking its toll. He still lived in cheap lodgings, not eating properly, his only luxury being cups of heavily sweetened tea. As he counted his profits and savings, he knew he was growing rich.

He permitted himself another luxury. Heinrich began

to send gifts to his father. It was not so much desire to be good to his father: rather it was as if he were saying to his father, "See, you rejected me—but I am successful." Along with the gifts he gave free advice, addressing his father as though the pastor were Heinrich's son!

The pastor enjoyed the gifts but ignored the advice. He was crotchety and had long since ceased to care what anybody said or did about him. He didn't bother to write to Heinrich.

Heinrich persisted with the letters for a while, constantly writing his father in such phrases as: "God would not have given me such success unless I deserved it."

Even the pastor realized Heinrich was becoming a prig. Isolated upon his lonely pinnacle of growing success, Heinrich was learning the love of command and power and the feelings of others seldom entered his plans. He became more and more of a financial machine.

As his buying and selling of indigo increased, it began to appear to Heinrich that he should be his own boss. He had helped Herr Schröder grow more wealthy and knew full well his own success was based upon the chance his employer gave him; however, the drive for personal wealth overrode all other things.

Such singleness of purpose as Heinrich showed brings returns. Opportunity does not hide from those who seek her. And while Heinrich was making up his mind about his next step, his opportunity came.

Herr Schröder had known for a long time that his chief correspondent was bargaining on his own in the indigo market. He did not mind, for Heinrich was faithful to the firm, and the deals did not upset Schröder's business. Nevertheless, Herr Schröder did not want to lose a good man. He summoned Heinrich to his office.

"Herr Schliemann," he said, "we have received an important offer of business, but it is in Russian and we cannot understand it. I have studied the possibilities and we have a great new market here if we can develop it. What do you suggest?"

Heinrich took the letter and turned it over in his hands. All his pride and bombast poured into his response. "Give me six weeks, Herr Schröder, and I will learn to read and write and speak Russian."

Even though Herr Schröder was now accustomed to Heinrich's methods of tackling a task, he raised his eyebrows. But what was there to lose? "Very well," he said, "and good luck to you."

Many Russians visited Amsterdam on buying trips, but Heinrich did not know any of them. The logical thing was to go to the Russian consulate.

"I need a teacher," he explained. "I will pay well. I must learn Russian as soon as possible."

The Russians had nothing to offer, so Heinrich left the consulate empty-handed. But he did not give up.

He succeeded in finding a Russian grammar and some books in Russian with stories which, in other languages, he knew by heart. By sheer force of concentration, dealing with familiar stories, he managed to make some sense out of the construction of the language. Using his dictionary, he once more made word lists and tried to attain correct pronunciation. He began seeking out merchants he thought were Russian in order to practice his growing knowledge of their language, but there were very few in Amsterdam. Most of those who visited the city could speak Dutch or French or some other language.

The need to practice, to get his tongue around and under the strange and difficult words, was great. He had to have assistance. Heinrich solved his problem neatly. He hired a poor old man to sit and listen to him. The man was glad of the work and it did not concern him that he didn't understand a word his employer was saying to him. He needed the small sum of money Heinrich paid him, so he listened.

Heinrich had this man come to his lodgings, night after night. Heinrich paced the floor, reading aloud the essays he had written, reading passages from the books and words from the dictionary. It satisfied him that he had some kind of audience. So noisy did these sessions become when Heinrich was carried away by his own eloquence, that neighbors complained and he was forced to move several times.

But he succeeded. A day or two before the six weeks had elapsed, Heinrich called on Herr Schröder. "I am ready," he said, "to handle any business from Russia that comes in."

Herr Schröder was nonplused. There could be no denying that this scarecrow of a correspondent was brilliant.

Within months, Schröder's was building substantial business with Russian merchants. Heinrich now took every opportunity to seek out Russian merchants, and he had more on his mind than making money for Schröder's. The Russian merchants were astonished to find someone who spoke their own tongue so easily and well, and Heinrich soon had many wealthy Russian acquaintances.

Rumor that Heinrich was planning to form a partnership with a wealthy Russian reached Herr Schröder. He was not ready to lose so valuable a man as Heinrich, so he moved first.

"Herr Schliemann," he said to Heinrich one day, "I have a plan I wish to discuss with you. How would you like to go to St. Petersburg as representative for Schröder's?"

Heinrich smiled inwardly.

"You will have sole charge of all Schröder's business

from all over the world in St. Petersburg," Herr Schröder went on. "Does that please you, eh?"

Heinrich accepted at once. This was too good a chance to miss.

Feeling very confident, Heinrich approached other firms. He sought to represent them, too, in the Russian city. He told them all that he would not take one penny of commission until he had proved to them that he could do good business for them. Most of them accepted.

Heinrich made ready for departure to the cold, snowbound city to the north. It did not bother him that he had never been there before, knew nobody there. His self-confidence was supreme.

CHAPTER 4

The Wanderer

THE JOURNEY Heinrich Schliemann was about to begin was to turn into a restless wandering over the face of the earth—a journey that lasted for a great part of his life. As his wealth multiplied, his restlessness kept a close parallel.

He wrote to his family glowingly and boastfully of the future ahead of him in Russia. They responded as if to a cold stranger, which indeed Heinrich had become. Only his brother Ludwig sought to take advantage of Heinrich's prosperity.

Ludwig wrote Heinrich, spelling out his desire to go into business for himself, and hoped his brother would put up the necessary capital.

Heinrich replied with a cold refusal. "The only way to succeed," he wrote, "is through your own efforts of concentration and skill. After all," he continued, "nobody helped me. I have had to get along as best I could without an education. I see no reason why you should not do the same."

48

The ingrained habit of self-denial made it easy for Heinrich to deny others. He seemed to have forgotten that if it had not been for the helping hand Herr Wendt offered him when the need was so great, he would not be enjoying his present prosperity.

About the middle of January, 1846, now twenty-four years old, Heinrich set out for St. Petersburg. He traveled as far as possible by train, then rode the rest of the way in whatever coaches, sleighs, or transport he could obtain. Railways had not yet connected the countries of Europe and Asia. Bundled in the warmest clothes he could find, Heinrich patiently bore the tiresome journey into the bitter cold. On the first of February, he rode into the fabled city.

St. Petersburg was then under the rule of Tsar Nicholas I. It had been founded by Peter the Great in 1703, on the river Neva. After his visit to European capitals, Peter wanted to westernize Russia, so he built his capital as close to the West as possible, moving the seat of government from Moscow. The city itself was to suffer as many ups and down as Heinrich Schliemann. In World War I the name was changed to Petrograd, because St. Petersburg was a German name and Russia was at war with Germany. After the Bolshevik revolution, the Communists changed the name again, this time to Leningrad.

When Heinrich Schliemann first saw it, St. Petersburg lay whispering under a heavy, glittering snow. He was very impressed by the houses and palaces of nobles and merchant princes that lined the Nevsky Prospekt, the finest street in the city. Immediately, Heinrich identified himself with this part of the city's life, and searched for quarters there. Perhaps it was through fear of being caught up again by poverty, one cannot guess. But Heinrich pretended to himself that the misery of serfs and peasants, the pitiful circumstances he saw all around, did not really exist. The pretense slowly turned into reality. He became totally unaware of the poverty of the people whom Tsar Nicholas ruled with an iron hand.

Heinrich soon saw that business prospects were even better than he had thought. He took to the Russian style of business dress. Sometimes he varied the high silk hat he wore with the astrakhan fur headgear so popular and warm. His thin lips were now partly obscured by a waxed mustache. On his pointed nose he wore gold-rimmed

Heinrich entering St. Petersburg.

spectacles. He adopted the ankle-length fur-lined over-
coat. The general effect made him look like a gloomy un-
dertaker planning his own funeral!

While he was able to ignore the poverty all around,
Heinrich could not help being amazed at the backward-
ness of Russia. The rest of Europe was stirring to the
Industrial Revolution, especially England. But Russia,
because of the blindness of Nicholas I and others, slum-
bered on in feudal ignorance. To Heinrich, all this simply meant a chance to develop his business. He stayed
at the best hotel, though, frugal as always, he booked the
cheapest room.

Heinrich set up his office and made himself known to
Russian merchants. Business was flourishing. By the end

Statue of Peter the Great, and the Bourse (stock exchange).

of the year, Herr Schröder wrote: "I am delighted with your progress. I now authorize you to deduct one per cent of all orders as your own commission."

Heinrich traveled to Moscow frequently. Whenever he heard of a merchant who was looking for goods, he did his best to find them for him—at a price. No deal was too small for his attention. He branched into all fields— indigo, spices, metals. Anything he could find that would bring him a profit, he handled, whether for Schröder or himself.

By 1850, Heinrich Schliemann was a millionaire!

His office was operating smoothly, so Heinrich set out on a tour of Europe, seeking to expand his own "empire." He marveled at the industrial development of England. The soot and dirt and filth left him unmoved. It was the tremendous factories of Birmingham and Manchester and other Midland towns that fired his imagination.

For a moment, young Schliemann was forced to pause. London's British Museum captured his imagination. He spent many hours there, staring at the array of Orien- tal and Greek and Roman relics. He experienced the first faint reawakening of his early desire to find Troy as he gazed upon these wonders of a long-dead past, but his time was not yet. He backed away.

Returning to St. Petersburg, Heinrich found that he had been elected a member of the Merchants Guild. It was recognition of his wealth and his solid position in trading circles.

Throughout these formative years, Heinrich had not developed a single intimate friendship. His relationships were all on a flat plane of business matters.   Now, with his new recognition as a man of importance in Russia, he began to feel the need to put down roots.   Perhaps, he thought, it was time to think of marriage.   So he began coldly to look among the merchants' daughters for one who might make him a suitable wife.   And from this moment, there began to sprout in his mind the seed of the thought that warned him that he was on an endless treadmill of money-making.   But he quickly stifled the flickering moments of awareness of his barren life.

Heinrich did not seem to understand that money cannot buy love.   He seemed blind to human values.   He did not know that while it might work to be coldly ruthless in reaching the top in business, it was an altogether different matter when dealing in emotions and human passions. He set about finding a wife in the same calculating way that had led him to a fortune.

Heinrich rarely smiled.   His eyes revealed signs of warmth only when he was working on a business matter. In truth, his emotions seemed as frozen in his heart as was his body frozen when he emerged from the bitterly cold sea of his shipwreck.   The price the little man paid was heavy.   Few girls bothered with him—he was such a peculiar fellow, and his wealth was not much help.   Still, he kept up his search.

In the early part of 1850, Heinrich received notice of an item in a California newspaper.   He knew that his brother Ludwig had gone there to seek his fortune, but he had long since lost contact with his family.   Once, Ludwig had written telling how well he was doing, but Hein-

Heinrich Schliemann in Russia.

rich had been too engrossed in his own affairs to pay attention.

The newspaper clipping reported that Ludwig Schliemann had died in Sacramento, of typhus fever. It was followed by an announcement that he had left a large fortune.

Heinrich was stunned. For the first time in years, the icy heart within him was pierced by grieving. He had not been close to his brother since they were children. Now, the streak of possessive love that was buried in his heart squeezed a few tears to sting his eyes. Childhood memories flooded back to torment him and he wallowed in self-pitying emotion.

Still, grief or not, the practical side of Heinrich's nature held the upper hand. Something had to be done about that fortune. He convinced himself that he was more concerned with seeing his brother's grave properly cared for than getting the money—but *somebody* had to go and claim the money, and he was the only one who could afford the journey.

By December, Heinrich settled his affairs in St. Petersburg and was ready to leave for California. He was eager to see the new land of America.

Heinrich had lived quietly and carefully, avoiding any show of lavishness. He saw himself as a typical, sober businessman, and acted out his role accordingly. Before leaving for America, however, he broke his rule of thrift and gave a large dinner party for his business acquaintances. It was not so much generosity as it was a way of assuring them that one day he would probably return. These contacts would always be useful!

Heinrich set out on the long, cold sleigh ride toward Germany. Perhaps, had he guessed what lay ahead, he would have shrunk from it in horror. Yet, when the adventures came, he met them with great courage and determination.

A few days before Christmas, 1850, he reached London. He exchanged his British letters of credit for letters of credit and introductions to American firms and businessmen. Then, he booked passage on the S.S. *Atlantic*, sailing out of Liverpool.

The S.S. *Atlantic* was a big ship for her time, and very fast. She was a side-wheel steamer, something new for Heinrich, and he boarded her, looking admiringly at her trim lines and appearance of strength and power. He enjoyed the thoughts of the difference between his boarding the *Dorothea* and his ability to buy such excellent accommodation as the S.S. *Atlantic* offered. In a few years he had climbed from a naked, frozen sailor to wealth that commanded service and deference from others. He found it pleasing to have such thoughts.

But the sea had never liked Heinrich, nor treated him kindly. The sea was as ruthless and impersonal as Heinrich had allowed himself to become.

Eight days out of Liverpool, almost in mid-Atlantic, the ship ran into bad weather. Enormous waves began to pound her, giant seas rose up like mountains and washed over the decks. A gale sprang up with great strength, adding to the pounding on the ship. She was

3,000 tons and strongly reinforced with iron plate, but it was little protection against the power of the sea. Seasick and frightened, Heinrich stayed in his cabin. He paced the floor, then fell roughly as the rolling of the ship threw him off his feet. He wrung his hands, crying, "Oh God! Is this to be the end of all my efforts? Is this the reward for all I have endured?"

A great wall of water loomed up from the ocean and bore down relentlessly upon the wallowing ship. Cries of fear rent the air and echoed around the decks. Tons of water hit her broadside, and when the water passed on the side wheels had been smashed to bits. The ship tossed helplessly out of control.

After this disaster, as if repentant, the weather eased. Heinrich forgot his seasickness in his anxiety over his predicament. He wondered what the captain would do. He was not long finding out.

The captain ordered his crew to hoist small auxiliary sails to the masts. He decided to fight his way on to New York. But the strong winds picked up again and the frightened passengers began to complain, afraid of the long journey ahead in such weather. The captain was forced to turn the ship around and return to England.

After sixteen days of struggle, the S.S. *Atlantic* made landfall at Queenstown, Ireland. Heinrich wasted no time returning to Liverpool and the next ship out. Messages waiting to be forwarded to him called him back to Holland on business matters. Like a frantic frog, he hopped to Holland, then back to England.

On the first of February, 1851, he again sailed for New

York, this time on the S.S. *Africa*. For once, the sea was
kind. The voyage was uneventful. Heinrich suffered no
illness or discomfort, and he arrived in New York in good
spirits.

Young Herr Schliemann was impressed by New York
City, and the size of some of the buildings amazed him.
He sensed a vitality about the people that caused him to
linger. He made good use of his introductions and after
meeting several bankers and businessmen he was firmly
convinced that the United States would grow into a tremendous power. His sharp business nose led him to investments in railroads, among other ventures, for he believed that these vital lifelines would soon crisscross the
length and breadth of the land. "It seems," he remarked
to a business acquaintance, "as if New York is the narrow
neck of a funnel. One can sense a great surge and whoosh
of life out into the great open spaces beyond, like a funnel
in reverse action."

Heinrich's introductions placed him among the top
level of New York society and business circles, and his
great wealth opened nearly all doors. He had no trouble,
even, in meeting President Fillmore. He was well received, to his immense satisfaction, and the free and easy
way of life in America, as he saw it, made a small dent
in his hard shell.

But California called, and his business there was the
reason for this visit. He was well content with what the
visit had led him into, and now he set about making plans
to travel to California.

There was then no Panama Canal, but the quickest

route to San Francisco was still by ship, and travelers in a
hurry crossed the Isthmus of Panama by land. It was
better than risking the dangerous seas around Cape Horn.

Heinrich sailed down the east coast of America. Long
before the port of Colón rose out of the sea ahead of the
ship, he could smell the lush tropical vegetation of that
steaming land. Fascinated, he watched the sea change
from deep blue to jade green as they worked their way
into port. He sniffed the rich warm air like a dog with
a fine bone. Tingling with excitement, he left the ship.

Heinrich had never seen anything like the sights that
now swirled about him. He took a quick dislike to the
native people, considering them lazy and dirty and shift-
less. He did not stop to realize that life in the tropics
was vastly different from northern lands he had always
known. He made no allowances. Disliking Colón so
much, he quickly joined a mule train that was due to cross
the Isthmus to Panama City.

The brilliant plumage of the bird life astonished him.
Wild orchids abounded among the heavy tangle of vines
and creepers. Each side of the narrow trail rose in a
solid wall of wild jungle growth. It seemed to threaten
the pathway for having intruded upon its mysteries. The
shrill cries and whistles and animal calls that echoed from
all around were eerie and startling to Heinrich. Immense,
colorful butterflies and weird-looking insects darted across
the path at every step. Monkeys called shrilly at the party
as it passed on its way. Bloodthirsty Indians lurked in the
darkness of vegetation, and Heinrich wavered between
fear of the tropical weirdness and admiration for its savage

beauty. He noted with horror that the Chagres River was alive with alligators. Fierce, vicious-looking creatures, he was sickened by the sight of them, and greatly relieved when the mule train emerged from the jungle and approached Panama City.

His archeological instinct was aroused when he visited the old city of Panama. It had been destroyed by the pirate Henry Morgan in 1671. As he scrambled about the ruins, Heinrich was intrigued to note how nature had already begun to bury the old ruins. Huge vines had worked their way between the bricks and blocks of stone that had once been buildings, tumbling walls and covering them with decayed matter until they were almost completely obscured.

Nothing else at Panama City interested him. It was as bad, he thought, as Colón, except that it was bigger. He was glad to find a ship, the S.S. *Oregon,* about to leave for San Francisco, and immediately booked passage.

Heinrich hated everything about the long and tiresome voyage. The food was bad and he had trouble keeping himself clean. He had grown very fastidious about his personal hygiene. The short stop the ship made at Acapulco, Mexico, did nothing to lift his spirits. His dislike for the natives was as strong as it had been at Panama. As he looked about him, he felt glad he had not gone to Venezuela aboard the *Dorothea.* How different his life would have been, but for that shipwreck! He felt sure Venezuela would be much like Panama and Mexico as he saw them.

Heinrich Schliemann had very little to say about San

Diego. The cluster of adobe buildings could hardly be called a port. Then his spirits rose as the S.S. *Oregon* approached San Francisco. Like so many others before and since, Heinrich Schliemann fell under the spell cast by this magic city on the west coast of America, inlet and outlet of the immense state of California, so recently joined to the United States.

CHAPTER 5

Gold, Death, and Jungle Terror

DELIGHTED though Heinrich was with his first sights of San Francisco, he immediately left for Sacramento. He convinced himself that it was desire to see Ludwig's grave properly marked that made for haste, but the biggest part of the haste was desire to get the fortune settled and safe.

When he arrived in Sacramento, he was struck by the fact that there seemed to be more graves in the graveyard than people living in the city. "Why is this?" he asked the keeper of the cemetery.

"Typhus," was the laconic reply. "It's the hidden enemy of the gold seekers. Far worse than any six gun!"

Heinrich found his brother's grave and arranged to have a marble headstone placed over it.

Wandering about the town, he learned that when Ludwig had arrived there Sacramento was little more than a ramshackle collection of huts and tents and wooden shacks. Now it was growing fast. Gold was bringing people in by the hundreds, and the town had a population of 20,000. Tradesmen and dealers followed hard upon the heels of those seeking the yellow metal.

Heinrich set about claiming the fortune his brother had left. Ludwig's partner had vanished. And the fortune had disappeared with him! Heinrich railed at the law officers, lecturing them on law and order. He threatened to call upon his friend, President Fillmore, if he did not get action.

Patiently, the law officers explained. "We have only just become a state. People are flocking here in thousands. It is impossible to keep track of everything. There is a vast wilderness between Sacramento, California, and Washington, D.C. Washington might as well be in Europe for all the aid it can give us here!"

There was nothing to be done; looking for Ludwig's partner was like searching for a black ant at midnight. Reluctantly, Heinrich accepted the obvious. He gave up the quest. Still, he had not come all this way for nothing. He determined he would not return to Europe empty-handed. The gold bug bit him. Opportunity was in the air and Heinrich could smell it. Sacramento pulsated with rough, wild life and hundreds poured in each day swelling the population, seeking gold. The exhilaration of the gold rush, the challenge of the wild country, captured him and would not let him go. A wise man, if careful, could make a fortune in a short time. But he would not make it, Heinrich thought, by digging with a pick and shovel or with a basin in which to wash gold nuggets from the earth.

Hurriedly, he made his way back to San Francisco, where he contacted banking houses such as Rothschild. New York and Washington quickly confirmed his credentials and the fact that he had vast resources at his disposal. The bankers accepted his credits and agreed to buy whatever gold he would send them.

Cautiously, Heinrich began his venture by making small loans. He grubstaked prospectors with the understanding that the loans were short-term—and with high interest.

Spreading his activities, Heinrich put up at a clean hotel, complaining at the overcharging. But accommodations were scarce.

On June 4, 1851, after a tiring but exciting and busy day, he retired for the night. Heinrich was aroused from a deep sleep by the clamor of warning bells and shouting in the street below. He jumped from his bed and ran to the window. The sight that met his gaze appalled him. A sheet of flame was tearing across the city.

All San Francisco was on fire!

Shadowy figures streamed through the street below, a weird picture as firelight picked out silhouettes of people dragging wagons and pushing carts. Horses screamed and neighed with wild fright. A strong wind carried the flames from one group of buildings to another, leaping wide streets as though they were nothing. Flimsy wooden buildings blazed like torches. A red, lurid glare, tinged with yellow, hovered over the nightmare scene.

As Heinrich watched with dreadful fascination, explosions added to the awful confusion. Police and soldiers were blowing up buildings, trying to create a barrier across which the searing flames could not reach.

Heinrich dressed hurriedly, ran downstairs and raced

up Telegraph Hill. He had no idea what he was doing, where he was going. He was caught in the panic with the rest. The screams and cries of hysterical people fleeing, or trapped in burning buildings, created a bedlam about Heinrich's ears. He saw sights that quickened even his icy blood. Rumor spread that "foreigners" had started the fire. Before his very eyes, Heinrich saw some unfortunates caught by the fury of the panicky mob slaughtered cruelly just because they were foreign. But there was authority at work, too, and the blaze was slowly brought under control. At the end, much of San Francisco was a charred ruin.

Heinrich was astounded at the resilience of the Americans. "The dregs of Europe" some snobbish people in the Old World called them. These people didn't look like dregs to Heinrich.

"What are you doing?" he asked one couple he saw poking about the ruins of a building, while it still smoked.

"No sense jest sittin' lookin' at it," said the man. "We'll jest start all over!" All around him, Heinrich saw similar sights.

Heinrich shook his head in amazement. As the cold gray dawn spread over the debris, men and women were already preparing to rebuild from the disaster. A new respect for these people took hold of Heinrich Schliemann.

As soon as he could, Heinrich set off for Sacramento. He moved into the strongest building he could find and purchased a heavy safe. Taking due note of the lawlessness, the violence, and murder in the wild gold fields, he bought a pair of pistols. Sanity and yellow gold, he knew, did not always mix well. It mattered not to Heinrich how odd he looked. He strapped the pistols around his waist over his banker's dress and wore them night and day.

From the beginning, Heinrich was successful as a buyer of gold dust and nuggets. As soon as his safe filled with the precious metal, he sent it off to San Francisco on the stagecoach. Then he started buying all over again. Each shipment brought him a handsome profit. He grabbed meals whenever he could snatch a few minutes, for he was desperately afraid to leave his office for a moment. He did not trust the assistant he employed.

And Heinrich paid the price. Fever took him, and he was racked with pain.

Still he would not give in. He dosed himself with quinine and, supplementing that with sheer will power, he carried on. His yellowish skin looked ghastly. He suffered three bouts of fever before his common sense took command.

He had made a vast amount of money, and it was time to leave. Heinrich went to the bankers in San Francisco. Liquidating most of his California assets, he found he had, in a short time, enriched his already large fortune by nearly half a million dollars!

Everything Heinrich Schliemann touched had turned to gold, yet restlessness nagged at his spirit.

The still-young man considered his next moves carefully. From time to time he wavered, torn between his desire for the individual and vital freedom he found among Americans, and the cultured part of his nature, which called him back to St. Petersburg. An elegant life awaited him in the Russian city he thought of as "home."

He decided to return and settle in St. Petersburg. He would find an aristocratic young girl and make her his wife. He still had vast investments and sums of money in Europe, and with his investments in America he could return whenever he wished. Heinrich booked passage on the best ship he could find and sailed for Panama, the first part of the journey back to Russia.

The sea was angry with him again. He found he had chosen the worst time of the year to make the voyage. High seas and strong winds battered at the ship all the way to Panama City. More dead than alive, Heinrich finally staggered ashore. Once his feet were again on dry land, he recovered quickly.

Inquiring about a mule train leaving for Colón, he was told: "Mule train many miles, señor." Vaguely, the native pointed in the direction of the jungle. "Rail train now goin' much into jungle. Pretty quick, soon go all way!"

Heinrich was delighted to find this true. The first section of a railroad across the Isthmus of Panama had been laid and was operating. Beyond a point several miles out of Panama, however, he would have to travel by mule train.

While waiting at the station for his train to leave, Heinrich wandered only a short distance from his luggage, for his bags contained all his letters of credit and hundreds of thousands of dollars in securities.

A native lurked suspiciously near. Fearfully, Heinrich seized his bags. The native followed him, and Heinrich could not tell if the inscrutable face was amused or threatening. Hurriedly, he bought a large knife which he stuck in his belt with his pistols.

Rain was pouring in torrents from the sky when the train reached the end of the line. Soaked to the skin, but clutching his bags tightly, Heinrich joined a mule train that was about to leave for Colón. He shrugged off the steaming rain. There was nothing he could do about it except endure it.

Swirls of vapor wrapped around the mules as the band of travelers entered the great green-walled jungle trail. They staggered on, alternately soaked by rain or soaked in their own perspiration.

Three days out on the trail, as though they sensed disaster, the native guides deserted the band of travelers. When they awoke in the morning, the travelers were alone. Their guides had taken all the food and water and the mules.

In the despairing discussion of their predicament, Heinrich sided with those who wished to go on. "We are no better off going back than in trying to reach Colón," he said. "Either way, we are equally lost. We can guide ourselves by the sun, and, who knows, we may soon meet another party coming this way. I shall go on to Colón."

The small group decided to struggle on. Rain con-

tinued to beat down upon them and they were soon hopelessly lost in the green hell. There was no means of lighting a fire to cook food. The monkeys and iguana lizards they shot or captured had to be eaten raw.

Staggering in the steaming heat, surrounded by lush green growth, the band was permeated with fear. Some swore they had seen hideously painted natives watching them from the jungle. Slowly, madness crept into their midst and the weak began to fail and fall by the wayside. Nobody paid them any heed. All a man could do was try to keep himself alive. Quarrels and fights broke out among members of the band. Some days no food could be found. Those who stumbled were left to die where they fell. There was no one to carry them. Each day, another one or two were missed from the band. Either they had been murdered by one of their companions or had fallen victim to Indians, snake bite, or worse.

During their rare pauses for rest, Heinrich dared not sleep. He seldom closed his eyes. He clutched his pistols fast and tied his luggage to his belt before he closed his eyes. Always he sat a little apart from the rest. He took no part in their talk, made no contribution to their plans. Survival was all that mattered, and he vowed that he and the fortune he carried would survive. He swore he would not be buried in the jungle.

Once, he stumbled and fell. Two ghastly figures waited above him, eager to see if he would rise. Heinrich rose, one hand on a pistol. But he had a bad gash on his foot, and before long it turned gangrenous. Dysentery added its ghastly pain to his sufferings, but he hobbled on, always several dozen yards behind the rest. Death and violence had been with him so long, it became natural and Heinrich ceased to feel its shock.

After fourteen pain-racked, terrible days of torment, the few survivors of the trek stumbled into Colón. Surrounded by clouds of mosquitoes, filthy, with straggly, lice-ridden beards, they sank their emaciated bodies to the ground. Heinrich still clutched his fortune.

Afterwards, Heinrich was never able to think or speak much about this terrible journey across the Isthmus of Panama, once he had recovered from his injuries. Courage and determination had enabled him to survive the jungle as it had helped him survive the business jungle. Incredible though it seemed to him, he had survived— but he tried to shut the experience from his mind.

When Heinrich Schliemann reached St. Petersburg, he settled down as if nothing had happened. But doubts of the value of his mad money-making stirred in his conscience. He stilled its nagging by plunging into a frantic search for a wife, and lost himself once more in business. He took a huge apartment and furnished it lavishly. He invited nobles and merchants who had daughters, carefully studying each prospective bride.

And he made a bad choice.

At first glance, and even upon investigation, Catherine Lyschin seemed to be everything Heinrich desired. She was dark, beautiful, aristocratic, and tall. Heinrich was vaguely disturbed that she had to lower her lovely head slightly to look him in the eye.

They were married on October 12, 1852. Soon, the shaky edifice of cultured elegance Heinrich had erected began to crash about his ears. Catherine, apparently, had little love for this odd man she had married, despite the fact that she bore him three children. Money had been the magnet. She was idle and uninterested in Heinrich and his affairs. Happiness for Catherine consisted in visiting back and forth with the elegant friends she had known all her life. They made mockery of her "money-mad" German, and Catherine enjoyed the joke with the rest.

Heinrich was powerless to help himself or Catherine. He had neglected the warmth of human relationships too long. He tried, in his agony, ordering her to love him, and this made matters worse. So many important human values had been lost to him in his devotion to money-making. He had failed to learn the simple lesson that, to be loved, one must first develop the ability to love, without thought of self.

Frustrated, bitter, more lonely than ever, Heinrich tried to assert himself the only way he knew. He tried to force Catherine to his will, he tried to buy her love and companionship. All his efforts failed. They had no common ground for conversation or companionship. Quarrels were frequent whenever they were together in the huge apartment.

Heinrich began to stay away from his wife, keeping to his own rooms and his office. In his despair, he grew frantic. He doubled and redoubled his business holdings, until his behavior resembled that of a headless chicken in a financial barnyard. He had no direction other than to pile money on money.

The Crimean War broke out in 1854, and Heinrich made another fortune dealing in chemicals. He showered Catherine with furs and jewels in an effort to draw her closer to him, and she accepted the gifts as her right, but would have no part of Heinrich. She cared nothing for his business nor did she bother to entertain the few acquaintances he brought to the apartment. She would not travel with him and was delighted when he was gone.

For seventeen long years this hectic pattern persisted. Everything Heinrich touched turned to money, and, equally completely, personal happiness eluded capture. Bitterly, he dreamed of America. He began to long for the freedom, the easygoing acceptance he had found there. The dream only added to his misery. He could have returned to America any time he wished, but Heinrich was too possessive. He hated to give up anything that belonged to him. And Catherine Lyschin was his property, he thought. So were his son and two daughters, but, unhappily, they added no warmth or happiness to the marriage, for Heinrich's possessive attitude toward them only drove them closer to their mother. Sometimes, Heinrich tried to write to his son of his feelings and accomplishments, but the aloofness and boastful manner of the writing did not produce the effect Heinrich demanded.

He traveled widely during these years and taught himself Swedish, Polish, and Danish. But the clamor of doubt grew louder.

What was money? He was no happier now than he had been as a poor grocery boy. There must be some purpose to life besides the struggle for more wealth. What was he to do with his life? Where had he gone astray?

Deep within his mind, thoughts of Troy and scholarship murmured. Heinrich shied away from them. He was afraid to look at that dream. It, too, might turn to dust and ashes. Perhaps it was true that the heroic figures he had so treasured in his childhood were only myths created by the poet Homer. So few illusions were left to Heinrich he feared to tamper with this one. He realized too well that it lived on, buried deep beneath the shell he had wrapped around himself. Seldom did he stop to realize that much of his unhappiness was of his own making.

But Troy beckoned like an irresistible warm flame. If he trod the road toward that flame, would he find Achilles, King Priam, Hector, Helen and Paris, waiting beside it to welcome him? Or would they vanish as he approached, ghostly wraiths to mock him?

These confusing thoughts buzzed in his head until Heinrich beat his head with his hands in a vain effort to quiet their insistence.

But the dream refused to fade.

CHAPTER 6

The Voice of Futility

HEINRICH SCHLIEMANN's world-wide financial interests were flourishing. He believed he would never again be poor, whatever happened in the world. Depressions might come and go, but shrewd Heinrich had spread his interests so widely he was sure of survival. Strangely, knowledge of this left a void in Heinrich's life. It was a gradual process, but the drive to make money began to slacken.

The voice of futility whispered mockingly, "Money, money, money! *For what?*" And behind that voice, so faintly, but growing louder, another whispered, "Troy, Heinrich. Troy! Find it, Heinrich, it *is* there!"

Fear of disappointment made Heinrich drag his feet. He hesitated. Slowly, however, his old love of scholarship and desire for worthy recognition began to fill the void within. Pretending to himself that it was a mere pastime, between travels he filled his hours studying books written in modern and ancient Greek. The deeper he delved into learning these languages, the more enthralled he became with their beauty. Admiration for the tenacity of the Greek people filled Heinrich's heart. Although they had endured more than three hundred years of Turkish domination, they had somehow managed to keep their language intact. The methods Heinrich worked out for himself previously served him again and he soon had a working knowledge of Greek. Once more he made long lists of words, building his vocabulary, and wrote essays for his own enjoyment and to practice his skill. He began to play with the idea of becoming a writer.

Still the voice of futility nagged at him. "You have all the money you want, Heinrich. Is this all there is?" Heinrich began to realize that there must be something more, and pondered what it might be. Days passed and he saw little of Catherine or the children. He ceased to care. And he knew he must find a purpose, some new goal in life. But what? He knew the business world, and had conquered it, but it was no longer satisfying.

A most happy event came to Heinrich's aid and helped still the voices in his mind. He met a Greek scholar, Theokletos Vimpos, who was studying at the seminary in St. Petersburg. Heinrich was overjoyed when Vimpos agreed to look at his essays, correct them, and assist his study of Greek. At first, Vimpos was flattered and amused by the attentions of the very wealthy Heinrich. Silently, he would listen to Heinrich pompously declaim on Greece.

"In the faces of your race," he would say, "is all the classic beauty and loveliness of one of the world's greatest people. In their names lives on the glory of their magnificent past. And who can say—despite their present misery—that they will not rise again to glory? For in their veins, remember, runs blood that has enriched mankind and fed him for centuries of his endeavor."

As Theokletos Vimpos began to understand that, beneath the pomposity, Heinrich was sincere with all his heart, the flattery and amusement turned into solid friendship.

Almost for the first time, a little of the ice around Heinrich's soul melted. A little happiness came into his life. With Vimpos he formed a small circle of friends who shared their interest in Greek. He frequently entertained them at gatherings in his large apartment. But Catherine would not join them. It was a happy interlude for Heinrich—and the die was cast!

All too soon, he was forced back to business. Reluctantly, Heinrich had to give attention to his interests. A depression toward the end of 1857, giving signs of being serious, demanded every bit of Heinrich's skill and knowledge to protect his "empire." He weathered the storm and emerged not one whit worse off than before.

With his mind freed again of business worries, the whispered call to Troy grew louder. Heinrich could not put it off any longer. But still fearing disappointment, he approached a trip to Greece in a most roundabout manner. Still trying to fool himself about the *real* purpose in his mind, in the summer of 1858 he completed plans to visit Greece. The pilgrimage had begun.

He started off through Scandinavia. Next, he spent a few days with his aging father in Germany, then continued to Italy. The frantic frog seemed more frantic than ever. He circled Greece, going first to North Africa. He sailed up the Nile in an Arab *dahabeah,* riding in the flat, bargelike craft as far as the river's Second Cataract, to seek relics of Egypt's pharaohs. His archeological instinct stirred at the wonders his eyes beheld. Still, he could not bring himself to go directly to Greece. He circled his objective like a cat stalking a bird.

He continued his journey, next visiting Petra in Northern Arabia. This mysterious pink sandstone city, carved in the living rock, held his interest for a while. His guides had little information to offer. Nobody knew what strange race had built Petra or lived in it. But there it was, staring with windowless eyes, just at the meeting point of the deserts of the Holy Land and Arabia. In some odd fashion its architecture looked almost like modern Victorian.

Heinrich continued to Jerusalem, but found little there to hold his interest.

At last, he could hold out no longer.

Athens was all his wildest dreams come true. The superb remains of the glory of ancient Greece filled his soul with peace and contentment. The introductions Vimpos had given Heinrich led him into scholarly circles and he basked in the compliments he received for his perfect mastery of both ancient and modern Greek.

Heinrich Schliemann had found himself. He decided to stay in Greece. With the same ruthless enthusiasm that had carried him to the top in business, he planned to conquer the academic world. But he still shrank from Troy, and settled down to write a book on Ithaca.

Business, however, could not so easily be sloughed off. It demanded his return to St. Petersburg.

After the warmth of Greece, Heinrich could not tolerate the cold of Russia. His heart had found its home in Greece, and he longed to follow it.

Heinrich attempted a compromise with Catherine. "Let us move to Germany," he said. "I will give you a fine house and you can return to visit Russia whenever you wish." He pointed out the many advantages of such a move, not the least being that while Catherine visited Russia, Heinrich could go to Greece.

Catherine only laughed. "You go to Germany," she said. "I am perfectly happy here. And as for those old ruins in Greece, I simply cannot imagine what you want with them."

Heinrich argued with her, pleaded and cajoled. He went from threats of leaving her penniless to offering her the moon. But Catherine was unmoved. Finally, Heinrich was forced to see that there was only one thing to do. They agreed to separate, to go their own ways. Catherine was to keep the big establishment in St. Petersburg and the children, and she would be provided with enough money to live as she pleased. Heinrich could see his children whenever he wished.

Heinrich was free to roam and wander, do what he liked. In 1863, he left Russia for good. He sold his Russian business interests and found that he was worth many millions of dollars. He spread this money carefully in many lands, making sure that his investments would continue to grow. He was surprised to discover, once matters were settled, that he enjoyed being free.

Like Don Quixote tilting at his windmill, Heinrich parried with Troy. The first pleasure of his new freedom soon wore off, and his affairs needed little attention; how best to break into and conquer the academic world was still the big problem.

Heinrich set off on a tour of the world. He thought he would pursue a writing career and begin, as many others had before him, by writing his comments and observations of the sights he witnessed. Passports and such documents permitting travel were not required in those days. Corrupt officials in poorly run countries fell over themselves to entertain the man from the West who was rich enough to buy the best of everything.

From North Africa, where he visited the ruins of Carthage, Heinrich made his way to India. He roamed all over India, from the teeming cities, which disgusted him, to the cooler slopes of the Himalayas. He could not understand people who permitted sacred cows and sacred monkeys to roam at will, making everything filthy, and he made no effort to understand. Beggars and ragged fakirs depressed him. The color, the romance, of India passed him by.

He visited little-known Java and Singapore, and in 1865 he reached China. Heinrich had no understanding of China and hated everything about it—until he reached the Great Wall of China. This was something he could

understand. His appreciation for the immense man-
made barrier was profound. Nothing would satisfy him
until he had climbed to the top of the wall to look across
the vast distances of land on each side of it.

Cruelty was no new thing to Heinrich, but he loathed
the sight of severed heads of thieves and bandits stuck on
pikes in the imperial city of the Empress Tzu Hsi, Pe-
king. Sickened by the things he saw, Heinrich could not
leave the tortured country fast enough.

In contrast to India and China, Japan fascinated him.
Only a dozen years before, the American Commodore
Perry had forced Japan to open her gates to Western
commerce. When Heinrich Schliemann saw Japan, it
was still largely the incredibly beautiful, splendid, barbaric, colorful land of olden times. He loved everything
about the country and the people.

Heinrich kept careful notes of the lands he visited. By
the fall of the year, he had tired of the Orient and was
anxious to settle down and begin his book.

He sailed for San Francisco, where he stayed long
enough to renew his acquaintance with some businessmen, then sailed on to Nicaragua. The frantic frog kept
hopping. He had no intention of crossing the Isthmus
of Panama again, nor did he relish the long and dangerous
journey around Cape Horn, so Heinrich made an uneventful trip across the semi-wild land of Nicaragua.
Then he sailed across the Caribbean Sea to the island of
Cuba, landing at Havana. He stayed long enough to
buy some property on the Cuban island.

By 1866, a forty-four-year-old millionaire, Heinrich

Schliemann found himself in Paris, the home of restless wanderers. He established himself in an elegant apartment on the Place St. Michel, overlooking the Cathedral of Notre Dame, and his restlessness slackened. The long wandering had given him some purpose. Despite his age, he enrolled at the Sorbonne as a student, hoping to win a degree. During his studies he finished and published his first book, *China and Japan at the Present Time*. It did not make much impression.

In the Paris of Emperor Napoleon III and the beautiful Empress Eugénie, Heinrich lived the life of a wealthy noble. The Suez Canal, built by the Frenchman de Lesseps, and soon to be opened, was the talk of the city. He made one more attempt to get Catherine to join him there, for he was lonely in the big apartment. Catherine was not impressed by Heinrich's descriptions of the elegant life of Paris and did not respond. Thus, Heinrich's Russian children remained strangers to him, and he to them.

Heinrich's studies at the Sorbonne were not enough to keep him fully occupied. He kept close touch with the financial world and bought a string of properties in Paris. The days were long, and the lonely nights even longer. Heinrich whiled away his life, constantly busy, yet always aware of the voice of futility as it grew more insistent within his soul. And it was only through a few lectures in archeology at the Sorbonne that he found impetus to force his steps, at long last, on the way to Troy.

The summer of 1868 was an especially hot one in

Ithaca, Greece, but it did not bother Heinrich Schliemann. There were no hotels on the Greek island, but he found decent lodgings and met a man who knew and loved the Greek legends as much as Heinrich himself. Together, they roamed possible sites for excavation, for Heinrich had decided to try digging for himself. Combining instinct with geographic and descriptive passages from Homer he knew so well, Heinrich chose to dig on Ithaca. Here, he believed, he might discover the marriage chamber of Odysseus and Penelope.

Odysseus was ruler of Ithaca, and it was with reluctance he joined Agamemnon and Menelaus in their expedition against Troy. Returning home from the campaign, Odysseus was shipwrecked off the coast of Africa and spent ten adventurous years wandering before he found his way home to Ithaca.

Penelope, the wife of Odysseus, waited ten years for her husband while he made the exciting journeys Homer chronicled in the *Odyssey*. During Odysseus's long absence, many suitors wanted to marry the lovely Penelope, saying her husband had surely been lost forever. To put off making a choice and to gain time, Penelope began the arduous task of weaving an elaborate and intricate web. She said she would marry when the web was finished. But each night she secretly unraveled what she had woven during the day, and thus continued to await the return of her beloved Odysseus.

Heinrich believed the truth of the ancient legends, so with a few workmen set about clearing the rubbish from the northeast corner of the site. Then Heinrich roughly marked out what he believed to be the proportions of the chamber and commenced to dig.

Heinrich's eagerness caused many obstacles to bestrew his path. He had no experience, and belief in what he hoped to find was not enough. In later years, when experience and criticism had taught him more scientific methods, he was more careful. Prime Minister Gladstone of England pointed out how much Heinrich grew as he learned his science. But during the earlier excavations, Heinrich failed to keep proper records. He did not note depths and positions of objects he found nor the general condition of the site in which he worked. Because of his lack of organized method, later archeologists had a great deal of laborious effort to evaluate, classify, and explain the work Heinrich had done and the value of the things he found.

For the first few hours, they found nothing; the heat began to oppress the toilers. Then, as the picks struck stone, excitement seized them. They gradually uncovered the foundations of a stone room approximately ten feet by fifteen feet. Surely, Heinrich thought, letting his eagerness run away with him, this was the room of Odysseus! Striking wildly into the earth with his pick, in a manner that would horrify a modern archeologist, Heinrich smashed into a vase and broke it to pieces. The vase was buried a few inches below the surface. Appalled by this mishap, he dug more carefully. He was glad he did, because before much more digging he had uncovered a group of twenty such vases. All these vases contained ashes and this led Heinrich to believe they must be funerary urns. Continuing his search, he found a small

Striking, Heinrich smashed into a vase.

clay female figure blowing on a double flute. Then a sacrificial knife came to light from its centuries-old hiding place in the earth.

If, indeed, these were funerary urns containing the ashes of Greek heroic figures, he had not found the marriage chamber of Odysseus he sought. Nevertheless, this immediate success confirmed Heinrich in his chosen profession. He left the brief digging fully convinced of the integrity of Homer, secure in the trust he had placed in the ancient poet. The few animal bones he found in this place seemed to prove that it was a burial chamber and the bones the remains of sacrifices. He was delighted and well satisfied with his first small expedition. Heinrich's excitement ran away with him and he speculated on the possibility that the urns might even contain the ashes of Odysseus and Penelope themselves. But there were no inscriptions giving clues to the origin or history of this burial chamber. He liked his own construction of the meaning of the funerary urns.

Being able to talk to the villagers of Ithaca in their own language with great fluency, Heinrich was well liked and popular on this first expedition. There were many emotional scenes when Heinrich would gather the villagers about him, then recite to them from memory, in their own language, the wonderful stories of their glorious past.

After he decided to cease digging on the site, he prepared to leave for Athens. The new purpose, archeology, held great promise of fulfillment.

Spurred on by his desire to excavate, Heinrich Schlie-

mann left for the plain of Troy, traveling by way of
Constantinople, and good fortune smiled upon him. He
met a man who proved to be of great value in the years
ahead, a man who shared some of Heinrich's theories.

An Englishman, Frank Calvert, had great practicality,
wide knowledge and understanding of the Turkish authorities, and some experience in excavating ancient
ruins. Eagerly, Heinrich explained his ideas and his
hopes to Frank Calvert as they made a tour of the plain.

At Bunarbashi, which some theorists believed might be
the site of Troy, Heinrich found only a huddle of miserable huts. The place was dirty and full of refuse, the
people ignorant, poor, a mixture of Albanians, Greeks,
and Turks. It was a far cry from the gleaming, beautiful
city of Heinrich's dreams. He did not, of course, expect
to find Troy resembling anything like what it had been
in its glory.

"But surely," he said to Frank Calvert, "this filthy
place cannot be hiding the palace of King Priam?"

"I am inclined to agree with you," Calvert said. "In
1822—that was the year you were born—Charles Mac-
laren published a treatise in England. He, too, felt that
Bunarbashi was not the site of Troy."

While they sat resting, Heinrich browsed through his
Homer. "Yes," he said finally, "Homer agrees with us.
Here he says that the Achaeans passed back and forth between their ships and the besiegers at the gates of Troy,
many times a day. We must be several hours march from
the sea here. The most likely place for the site, it seems
to me, is the big mound at Hissarlik. That is not a

natural mound and it is much closer to the sea. Besides, I see not the slightest trace of a ruin at Bunarbashi."

Frank Calvert not only agreed with Heinrich, he actually owned part of the site containing the mound. He escorted Heinrich to Hissarlik, and showed him the two trenches he had dug himself. Calvert had hoped to publish his findings and interest the British Museum in sending funds and assistance. He did not have the unlimited funds Heinrich could call upon, so his efforts had come to nothing. Still, Frank Calvert was not a man to stand in the way of another. He willingly and freely offered Heinrich access to the portion of the site he owned.

"But," he said, "you will have to haggle with the owners of the other portion."

Heinrich could hardly credit the attitude of Frank Calvert. This gentle man was a true scholar, and he asked nothing for himself. Neither a share in the glory if the venture succeeded, nor payment for use of his land. Heinrich was extremely grateful.

Listening to the excited Heinrich, Calvert cautioned patience as he passed along his knowledge of the area and advice on the best times for work. Calvert pointed out the many things that must be done before any digging commenced. First of all, Heinrich must obtain a *firman* (permit) from the Turkish authorities. The site lay within their jurisdiction and nothing could be done without a permit. Usually, they were reluctant to grant them.

"But the Turkish government cares nothing for these old ruins," Heinrich insisted.

"That is not the point," Calvert reminded him.

"They do have control over this land, and if you find anything of value, they will soon show interest! If you work
without permission, trouble will surely follow and beset
you with any discovery you may make. Better to avoid
it, I'm sure, from the first."

Frank Calvert pointed out to Heinrich that the season
for digging was past. "It is best to proceed carefully," he
explained. "Do not arouse too much interest from grasp-
ing officials. Prepare quietly to obtain a permit to dig.
If you bide your time until next spring, the ground will
be in excellent condition for digging and you will have
all the time till then to work on obtaining the permit."

Frank Calvert's advice was sound and wise, and Heinrich, forcing himself to curb his exuberance and desire
to get to work at once, decided to follow it. Before returning to Paris, he made one more survey of the mound
at Hissarlik. Also, after Frank Calvert left, Heinrich
studied Homer anew, and made a brief survey of Bunarbashi.

Homer told of two springs at Troy which watered the
citadel. At Bunarbashi, Heinrich found over *thirty*
springs and was assured there were even more. This was
one more reason for deciding against Bunarbashi. At
Hissarlik, he did not find *any* springs, but, strangely, this
did not disturb him.

Heinrich remembered how Achilles, in his duel with
Hector, chased Hector around the fortress three times,
while all the gods looked on. This was according to the
tale as told by Vergil, the Roman poet, in his *Aeneid*.
Homer, in the *Iliad*, reported how Achilles dragged
Hector's body from the field of battle to the Achaean

ships. In his own mind, Heinrich could believe and visualize both events. Heinrich reasoned that Bunar-bashi was over fifty miles from the sea, and he *knew* the Achaeans could not have made that journey back and forth from their ships "several times a day." He was satisfied with the accuracy of Homer.

Carefully timing himself, and checking in his Homer all the while, Heinrich paced out the road between the two hills of Troy. Even though Troy had been destroyed over three thousand years before, Heinrich became more convinced than ever that beneath the mound at Hissarlik he would discover the huge walls described by Homer and depicted so graphically in the book he had loved as a boy. He sat down and put his mind to re-creating the scene as it might have been during the siege of Troy. And his belief became unshakable. The mound of His-sarlik was flat on top, and when he paced its dimensions, Heinrich found it to be almost eight hundred feet long.

Hissarlik entranced Heinrich Schliemann. As he de-scribed it: "No sooner has one set foot on Trojan soil than one is astonished to see the noble mound, which seems to have been intended by Nature to be the site of a great citadel. If well fortified, the site would command the whole plain of Troy. In the whole region, there is no point that compares with this one. From Hissarlik, one can see Mount Ida, from whose summit Jupiter looked down upon the city of Troy."

Heinrich considered the ancient historians. Herod-otus told how Xerxes had visited the city of Troy. Xeno-phon had told of the visit of Mindares, the Lacedaemonian soldier. Arrian had told of Alexander the Great visiting the ruined city, and making sacrifice in his humility and admiration. Caesar, too, had been there.

The geographical and physical descriptions of these historians of the ancient world were too similar to Homer's to be ignored, in Heinrich's opinion. Alexander the Great, indeed, had been so moved when he first saw the ruins of Troy, he stripped naked, oiled his body, ran thrice around what was left of Troy in emulation of Hector, then made a sacrifice to the spirit of the dead hero. Caesar made an effort to restore some of the ruins. But when Heinrich saw the site, remembering the descriptions of the ancient writers, he was convinced that Hissarlik fitted in with them. Time had done its work and the site had changed much. But from his soul, Heinrich could gaze about the site, superimposing the pictures of Troy in its original splendor—then as it passed through the slow stages of its decay down through the ages—to the actual condition of it that met his eyes.

Could all the historians have been wrong about the location of Troy? Heinrich did not think so. He decided to believe them and let them, with Homer, be his guides.

Satisfied with his survey, Heinrich contacted Frank Calvert. Calvert, while not agreeing with all Heinrich's reasoning, believed he was largely correct. He promised to do whatever he could to hasten the permit. He gave Heinrich a long list of tools he should have and agreed to meet his friend the following spring. Content, Heinrich returned to Paris.

CHAPTER 7

The Iceberg Melts

PRODDED BY MEMORIES of glorious Greece, Heinrich plunged headlong into capturing his feelings on paper. He wrote a book, in English and German, describing his experiences and theories of the summer. The book was published in Leipzig.

Meanwhile, Heinrich had received word that he might be able to arrange for a divorce from his Russian wife, so he reluctantly planned to leave for America early the following spring. True, he might have to delay his excavating, but there were many ways he could rationalize such a decision. Away from Greece, now, fear of being wrong about Troy dampened his ardor. He was frightened by how little he knew of the mechanics of such excavating. Yet, had not the summer's excavating given him some firsthand experience?

Perhaps that's it, Heinrich thought. *I* know I can be a successful archeologist, but without the usual formal education, degrees and titles, who would take me seriously?

With characteristic determination, once a decision was made, Heinrich vowed to get the necessary titles and degrees. Once more, the nagging need for acceptance gripped the restless Heinrich, and his energies poured into getting his doctorate. Impatient and dissatisfied, now that he began to crystallize a new purpose for his life, Heinrich gave up his classes at the Sorbonne. He felt that it would take too long to earn the doctorate he so desired. Instead, he offered his thesis, the story of his life written in Classic Greek, to the University of Rostock. So long ago, it seemed, he had wanted to go there. He was delighted when they accepted this offer and awarded him his degree in the fall of 1868.

Heinrich was proud of being a Doctor of Philosophy. But like so many men who have had to struggle against great odds, he was terribly sensitive about his degree. He insisted, once he had earned it, that everyone address him as "Herr Doktor Schliemann."

Very early in 1868, Heinrich hurried to Indianapolis on business, and hoping to get his divorce there. His friends in Indiana assured Heinrich it would be easier for him to get a divorce in America and they promised to do everything possible to speed the legal processes. Though Heinrich expected immediate action, he did not receive it. Delay followed delay, until finally Heinrich wrote to his friend Calvert bemoaning the fact that the much anticipated digging would have to be put off until the next year.

Schliemann was hardly idle in America, however. He had large holdings in the United States which demanded attention, and he purchased a home in Indianapolis where he lived in elegance and style.

Who can say what quirks of nature dictate a man's action? It was an unusual quirk, indeed, which prompted one of Heinrich's decisions while awaiting his divorce.

Taking pen in hand, Heinrich wrote a lengthy letter to Theokletos Vimpos, in Athens, the only man he wholly trusted. He unburdened his heart to his friend. He asked him to search for a girl of good Greek background. Heinrich hoped, in this strange fashion, to marry a Greek and identify himself forever with Greece.

In a surprisingly short time, a reply reached Heinrich, and it contained several pictures, with accompanying descriptions. For Heinrich, there was but one. It was a photograph of a very beautiful Greek girl. Heinrich discarded the others and stared, with his piercing eyes, at the face which looked at him from the photograph.

Impatient, now that he had yet another purpose in returning to Greece, Heinrich did everything within his power to expedite his divorce. The wheels of the law, however, revolve slowly, and it was August before Heinrich finally reached that state of freedom he so much desired.

Heinrich felt he had a right to American citizenship, having been in California close to the time California became a state of the union. However, he went through the formalities of making his status in America legal. It is very likely that his purpose was to make doubly sure of his divorce. But this action, too, took time. For practical purposes, not idealism, Heinrich was truly a world citizen. On more than one occasion, to gain his own end, he used whatever nationality best suited his purpose.

Hardly daring to believe the truth of the beautiful girl in the picture, Heinrich nonetheless reached Athens in high spirits. He was delighted to be with Theokletos Vimpos again. Vimpos had now become a bishop and also a professor at the University of Athens. Here was one man who could understand the oddities of Heinrich Schliemann. Yet they talked of trivialities while Heinrich nibbled at the edge of the matter that brought him to Athens.

Suddenly, he burst out. "Tell me truthfully, is she as lovely as the photograph? Is she what I want? Does she come from good Greek stock? Is she educated at all?"

Vimpos laughed and held up his hand. "Steady, my friend. One point at a time." Vimpos assured Heinrich that Sophia Engastromenos was exactly the girl he wanted. He promised Heinrich she would make him a good wife. It was an old custom to arrange marriages in Greece, and this would be no exception. Vimpos explained that Sophia and her family had been told of Heinrich's interest in marriage, and although Sophia was just past sixteen, her family favored the union.

From excitement and enthusiasm, Heinrich plunged into doubt and worry. Extreme as always in his reactions, he refused to believe that anybody could be as ideal as Vimpos's description of Sophia suggested. Nevertheless, when he left his friend, it was with arrangements made for his first meeting.

With beating heart, chills tingling his spine, and sweat dampening his forehead, Heinrich arrived at the small village of Colonus, about a mile north of Athens. He chuckled to himself. Surely it was a good sign? Colonus, where Sophia lived, was the birthplace of Sophocles, a tangible link with the ancient Greeks he adored.

Sophia's family received Heinrich with great kindness and courtesy, and when they sent for Sophia to present her to Heinrich, his heart stood still. Not only was Sophia pure Greek stock, she had all the classic beauty of the Greeks. Never, he thought, had he seen anything so lovely as the dark beauty before him. Her voice was soft, warm, and musical. She moved with grace, was polite, and seemed eminently sensible. She accepted her family's plans for her future without question. It was impossible, Heinrich thought. Nobody could be so nice. There must be a flaw. There had to be a catch in it somewhere. Perhaps it was only his money they were seeking? But the dark beauty held him fascinated. During the courtship, Heinrich subjected Sophia to every test he could think of, hoping to find the flaw somewhere, yet dreading he would. He gave her written tests to discover the extent of her knowledge. He questioned her on character and virtue, asking all manner of things that were really impertinent.

Sophia smiled at him. Patiently, she answered the questions of this odd-looking man who wanted to marry her. She treated him kindly, sensing his terrible loneliness. And she passed his every test with ease and success. Sophia was not in the least disturbed by the difference

Never had he seen anyone so lovely.

in their ages. She found Heinrich a most pleasant
person.

The more Heinrich saw of her, the more he fell under
the spell of the Greek girl, until he was truly in love with
her. Timid, shy, desperately afraid of his great good
fortune, Heinrich was a long time in coming to believe
the truth. Habits of a lifetime are not easily broken.

After their marriage, on September 24, 1869, the
Schliemanns took a leisurely tour of Europe. Slowly,
Heinrich's eyes opened wide. The iceberg began to
melt. His beautiful Sophia—so much younger, so warm,
and so kind to him. "Dear God," he murmured, "a
miracle! This wonderful girl really loves *me*, Heinrich!"

All the love, the tenderness and passion he had bottled
within himself poured out to Sophia. Happiness burst
over him like a glorious sunrise.

They finally settled in a large house in Paris, and
Heinrich's cup was brimming over. He was lucky indeed
that Sophia honestly loved him. She bore patiently with
his frantic urging that she continue her education, and
he set her to learning French and German at the same
time, to be followed by English. Sophia did her best
and somehow succeeded in keeping Heinrich and herself
on an even keel between the violent extremes of his
nature.

So strong did the love become between this unusual
couple, there seemed to be almost a holiness in their re-
gard for each other. Two children were born to bless the
union. Proudly, Heinrich named the first, a girl, An-

dromache, after the wife of Hector of Troy.   The second,
his son, he named Agamemnon.   Heinrich's happiness in
his family was complete.

The strain of forced studying and the cold and damp
of Paris made Sophia ill.   She did not respond to the
elaborate medical care Heinrich obtained for her.   She
was pining for the warmth of Greece, so Heinrich took
her home.   He loved her too much to risk her health,
and felt guilty because he had burdened her with too
much study at one time.   They returned to Athens.

Finding himself once again in the shadows of the
glorious ruins of ancient Greece, Heinrich knew he must
answer the call of Troy.   Sophia was recovering rapidly,
and she urged her husband to follow his destiny.

"I am getting well, Heinrich, and there is no need for
you to worry about me.   I tell you I shall be all right.
You go, do what you must.   When you come back, I shall
be waiting for you here."

Heinrich took Sophia's lovely face between his hands.
The smile that came more and more readily to his poker
face creased the corners of his eyes.   "God bless you,
Sophia.   You are so good to me."

Now that his mind was made up, strengthened by his
recently won doctorate, Heinrich began his venture with
all the mad scrambling activity he had used in business.
The road to Troy was open to him.   But old fears of disappointment and disillusion died hard, and still he
hedged.   He decided not to go directly to Troy.   He
would be patient.

With copies of the *Iliad* and the *Odyssey* in hand, he

roamed the sites of ancient Greece. When Heinrich Schliemann plunged headlong into archeology, the systematic, careful methods used by scientists today had not been established. What little field work had been done had been undertaken by a few amateurs and novices. Many fancy and elaborate theories had been built upon the findings thus obtained—mostly by men who seldom visited the sites themselves. The countries which held ruins of ancient civilizations in their soil were unaware of or uninterested in using government funds to restore them to a place of dignity.

Heinrich Schliemann, in his own person, was about as unlikely an heroic figure as could be imagined. But what counted lay in the heart and in the mind. And here, with Sophia encouraging him and sharing his interest, he had all that was needed.

There was still no sign of the permit to dig at Troy which Frank Calvert had hoped to obtain for Heinrich from the Turkish authorities. Fuming and fretting over the delay, Heinrich thought to do some preliminary work at the ruins of Mycenae—but alas! a short time before, a party of English archeologists had been murdered by bandits in the area and the Greek government was reluctant to allow others to roam the site. There was nothing to do but wait for the permit from Turkey. Heinrich spent his time making short explorations of the Greek isles.

Heinrich's appetite for Troy was again whetted when he succeeded in buying some ancient vases from villagers he visited on various islands. He carried them to Sophia in Athens, explaining how they had been found buried under several layers of volcanic lava. But his excitement was tempered by annoyance when he returned home, for there was still no sign of the permit.

"Do not worry so, Heinrich," Sophia soothed him. "The *firman* is sure to arrive soon."

Heinrich kissed his wife. "My dear," he told her, "I could not bear such delays were it not for you." And Heinrich spoke truly and justly.

CHAPTER 8

Cross, and Double Cross

IN APRIL, 1870, Heinrich arrived at Hissarlik. Spending money lavishly for tools and equipment, he made ready for digging. He examined Frank Calvert's trenches, considering the position of the mound, and concluded that the western portion of the mound was likely to reveal the most promising remains. The height and general massiveness of this part of the mound seemed to Heinrich most promising. The larger the building that was covered, the larger the mound would be. And always the palaces and temples of ancient cities were the largest buildings.

This particular portion of the great mound belonged to two Turks who lived in a town a short way off, but Frank Calvert had been unable to reach any agreement with them to sell their land although Heinrich offered a good price.

"Very well," said Heinrich, "I'll deal with them if and when it becomes necessary."

Expecting to receive his permit to dig at any time now, he hired some workmen and began to dig, believing that once he had shown that buildings were buried beneath the mound, the Turkish authorities would not hamper his progress.

Leading his workers to the site, with his pistol at his waist, Heinrich set them digging at the northwest corner of the mound, where, he believed, he would uncover one of the ancient gateways of Troy. After the workmen had dug into the soft earth to a depth of two feet, they struck great blocks of stone! It proved to be part of a wall. With a peculiar mixture of eagerness and caution, Heinrich urged the men on. He hopped about them frantically, sometimes seizing a pick or shovel and getting in the way. By the time dusk arrived, they had uncovered ruins of what proved to be a building 60 by 40 feet.

It was too small, Heinrich thought, to be King Priam's palace, but Heinrich's enthusiasm shot up like a mercury thermometer. The next day he hustled around the villages hiring peasants until he had doubled his work force. Like a general leading his army, he took them to the site and deployed them to their tasks. Some of the extra men were set to digging at the south corner of the building that slowly emerged from the debris of centuries. Soon they reached the paving stones of the ruin. Nothing of any value had been found. The top layer of debris was made up of earth and decaying matter that had slowly built up by a combination of natural process and the habits of man.

The next step was to go beneath the stones of the paving. Now, Heinrich began to discover what he expected and hoped to find. Like a stinging gnat, he urged the men to care and caution, yet he himself tugged frantically at stones or picked rashly at the ground. Burned matter began to come to light beneath the paving stones. Studying it, Heinrich noted the burned and calcined material was in tight and orderly layers. Since stone did not burn, Heinrich decided that several wooden structures had once probably stood there which had been destroyed before the stone building had risen upon the ruins.

With great excitement he picked up a Roman coin in the cinders. One side of this coin bore the head of the Roman Emperor Commodus, and on the other side was the head of great Hector, son of King Priam! Heinrich knew it was Hector for the likeness carried the inscription "Hector Ilieon" (Hector of Troy).

Heinrich had hardly hoped for conclusive proof of the correctness of his theories so soon. He accepted this coin at once as proof that he was close to the remains of the citadel of King Priam, and his eagerness knew no bounds. Like a man possessed, he hurried on the work. Adding to his frantic haste was the knowledge that gossip of what was going on must now have reached the ears of the two Turks who owned the land. He was expecting them to turn up at any moment and order him off.

Hoping to gain some idea of the layout of the buried city, he ordered trenches dug in the Turkish-owned portion of the mound. One ran east and west, the one already made north and south. By slicing into the mound in this manner Heinrich reasoned that the trenches were bound to cross streets and houses and reveal where the most important buildings were likely to be grouped. Much carelessness resulted from Heinrich's haste and lack of archeological experience, but this method was correct and sound in concept. He thought it would avoid a good deal of unnecessary labor and effort and digging in wrong places, once he had an idea of the layout of the city.

Unfortunately for Heinrich, he had hardly begun this work when the two Turks *did* arrive. They were most annoyed to find him digging into their land and making such a mess, and they made all manner of dire threats to him. Vainly, Heinrich pleaded with them to let him remain and continue the work. He told them he was doing a great honor to their country and that all the world would be delighted when his discoveries were known.

All his guile and cunning served no purpose, however, for the Turks were not in the least interested. Heinrich offered them a high price for their land, much more than it was worth, but they held out for twice as much again. Heinrich wavered between his good business sense and his desperate desire to own the site and dig for Troy in peace; but his ingrained habits of dealing in the market place would not permit him to allow himself to be robbed.

Noticing the Turks eying the huge blocks of stone he had uncovered, a crafty look came into Heinrich's eyes. "The stones interest you?" he asked.

The Turks quietly mumbled together a while. "Yes," one of them said. "And rightly they belong to us. We wish to use them for a building we want to put up."

It was wrong, and Heinrich knew it. But after all,

he thought, in themselves the stones are not particularly significant. A few of them would hardly be missed.

He made an agreement with the Turks. Heinrich would let them take enough stones for their building if they would let him continue to dig. If they did not agree, he told them, he would have to report everything to the authorities, for it was an historic site they owned. They agreed.

Swallowing his sense of outrage at being forced to commit this crime with stones of great antiquity, Heinrich let them carry off the stones. Sadly, he realized that if he were to accomplish anything, he had little choice, and his eagerness allowed him to rationalize the crime. To keep them at peace and to buy more time, he added a small sum of money to the bargain.

Heinrich, in order to enlist support and interest from abroad, while hoping for his permit to arrive, published the news of his discoveries in a German paper. Some of the claims he made for the truth of the existence of Troy under the mound of Hissarlik were rash. He had very little evidence except "Hector's coin," a few potsherds, and the great stone walls. But this report was very truthful and frank, even to admitting that he began his digging without permission. He justified this by pointing out that the land was not being used for any purpose and he had tried to buy it for a good price. He said his work was of tremendous importance to archeology and that his discoveries made it imperative for the work to continue.

Heinrich hoped, through this article, to build up enough pressure to ensure that a permit would be

granted. His extravagant claims were not entirely ac-
curate, but his eagerness blinded him to the facts. Critics
immediately seized upon this, not bothering to examine
what truth there might be to Heinrich's claim, despite
his extravagance. They ridiculed him as an upstart, un-
scholarly amateur. This was easy enough to do from
their comfortable armchairs, and they did not bother to
go into the field and examine what evidence there was.
Heinrich did his best to ignore them. He was personally
satisfied that Troy was real and not the myth so many
scholars claimed it to have been. He had found it!

Unhappily for Heinrich, the Turkish authorities read
his report and were very angry with him. They determined not to let him continue his digging. He offered
as much as a hundred pounds, an enormous sum in that
area in those days, to the two Turkish landowners, but
they would not sell. They believed they had the measure
of Dr. Schliemann, and that eventually he would pay the
sum they demanded. Further, they claimed the hundred
pounds as compensation for the damage Heinrich had already done to their land. Angrily, Heinrich refused to
pay.

Heinrich vowed he would not let his work come to an
end through the ignorance and perfidy of the landowners,
and he almost became ill with his intense feelings over
the matter. Sophia was almost powerless to calm him.
The best she could do was to see to it that he ate and slept,
and she tried to keep unnecessary bother away from her
fuming husband.

Heinrich wrote letters to many of the most important

and powerful people he knew. He explained his progress and outlined his hopes for future work. He was convinced of Priam's Troy. It *did* await him—but prodigious effort only brought more criticism upon his head.

"I am tired, Sophia," he said one day. "The inactivity of Athens is depressing me. Troy is waiting for me, I know."

"Why don't you take a holiday, Heinrich," Sophia replied. "Perhaps Paris will refresh your spirit and give you an opportunity to relax and clear your thoughts."

"Yes, I think I will do that, Sophia. I have been wanting to look over my houses anyway. It is a good idea, my dearest, and I shall go."

Heinrich's hope for a pleasant summer was shattered. War broke out in July, 1870, between France and Prussia. Soon, the Prussians were at the gates of Paris, preparing to enter and occupy the city. Heinrich left hurriedly. He had no desire to be penned up in an occupied city.

Idling at Boulogne-sur-Mer, Heinrich could think only of Troy. The tragedy of Paris seemed to be of no consequence. When an acquaintance taxed him for callousness, he replied, bitingly, "Never fear, this will pass and the turn of the Prussians will surely come."

It was useless, Heinrich thought, to waste any more time idling. Obviously his letters were not going to be of any use in bringing pressure to bear upon the Turkish authorities. He decided to try direct action.

He left Bolougne and, in August, arrived at Constantinople. Immediately, he gained an audience with

Safvet Pasha, the Turkish official in charge of requests such as Heinrich's. Heinrich brought to bear all his mass of business cunning in his attempt to get his permit. He tried to get Safvet Pasha to intervene and force the land-owners to accept his good offer for the land at Hissarlik.

Safvet Pasha was just as cunning as Heinrich. He sat listening to Heinrich and reflected upon his conversation. He had not the least interest in Troy as an historical site of great importance, yet there was the possibility that this madman in front of him might find valuables. At least, he was spending money lavishly and employing peasants who needed the work. One never knew what might come of such things. Yes, indeed, this was a matter worthy of some thought.

The meeting was cordial, and Heinrich was promised the permit. Safvet Pasha assured him he would try to get the owners of the land to sell their part of the site at a reasonable price.

In high spirits, Heinrich notified Frank Calvert of his success, then waited for his permit.

Nothing happened until January of 1871. Then, after inquiries, Heinrich discovered the maddening truth of Safvet Pasha's cunning. The Pasha had forced sale of the land all right. But the title had been given to his depart-ment of the government, not to Heinrich as he had promised. Heinrich was told he could have permission to dig at his heart's content. It was all right with the authorities for him to spend as much of his own money as he chose. In these circumstances they would not hamper him.   But . . . anything of value he dug up from the ancient city of Troy would belong to the Turkish government!

Heinrich was even more furious when he learned that Safvet Pasha had paid little more than half the price for the land Heinrich had been prepared to pay.   With great indignation, he swept out of Constantinople and returned to Athens.

If Safvet Pasha thought he had got the better of Heinrich Schliemann, he was due for a surprise.

In Athens, other matters served to distract Heinrich, temporarily, from his concern over Troy.   He heard dreadful stories of the destruction caused in Paris by the Prussian soldiers.   "Sophia," he said, "I must return to Paris at once."

"But you can't, Heinrich!   It is terribly dangerous and unsafe there!"

"I must go, Sophia.   What of my property in the city? I must see for myself what has happened.   Besides, do not forget I can claim to be a German.   I know many important people who, I am sure, can get a safe-conduct for me.   Also, while I am there I will try again to enlist the aid of my powerful friends to shake Safvet Pasha from his position.   He will not, I promise you, get the better of me!"

"Very well, Heinrich.   If you are determined to go, then you will go, I am sure of that.   Only, please, my dear, please be careful.   I could not bear it if anything happened to you."

Heinrich's task was not easy.   He was well received,

for he was a man of great substance and property, but he ran into a stone wall. Nobody was allowed into Paris—not until peace had been declared. Heinrich appealed to the great Bismarck himself, but still he was refused permission to enter Paris.

He would not be put off. Fearlessly, Heinrich made plans and arrangements. He purchased, by bribes, a false German pass into the city. Ignoring the risk of being caught and shot as a spy, he boldly crossed the German lines, waving his pass at anyone who stopped him, talking rapidly in perfect German until, bewildered, they allowed him to pass. Heinrich spoke with great authority and, drilled as the Prussian troops were to blind obedience, lacking any personal initiative, they let Heinrich through to Paris.

The Paris that greeted him was a great relief. The stories of destruction he had heard in Athens were not true. Paris, except for the occupying soldiers who were everywhere, looked much as it always had. His property had not suffered much damage and his affairs were in good order. A great relief flooded him, quickly followed by an equally great determination. Now he could concentrate upon the wily Turk!

Heinrich began to write letters to Safvet Pasha, craftily agreeing to share half of any treasure he should find at Troy. In the meantime, having failed to obtain any worthwhile support in Europe for his work, he decided to assert his right as an American citizen.

It was fortunate for Heinrich that he did so, for the American Ambassador to Turkey proved to be a man of

Heinrich led Sophia over the site of Troy.

great learning and culture, with great knowledge of Homer.

Heinrich's sincerity and enthusiasm infected the Ambassador, who became convinced that Heinrich was on the verge of highly important discoveries of value and worth to the whole world.

Together, Heinrich and the Ambassador wrote letters to Safvet Pasha and arranged further meetings with him. With so powerful a backer as the American Ambassador, Heinrich found Safvet Pasha more amenable. They quickly reached a satisfactory agreement and Heinrich was promised a permit just as soon as it could be signed and delivered to him.

Heinrich was visiting England in August of 1871 when a heavy sealed envelope was delivered to him. Feverishly, he ripped open the bulky packet. He was overjoyed to behold the permit which had caused him so much trouble. Instantly, he started to pack, then dashed off to the shipping agent to arrange his passage.

Fate was kind to Heinrich now. Sophia was in excellent health, and, with the eagerness of a child, Heinrich took her by the hand and led her over the site of Troy. He explained what had been done so far, and what he was now proposing to do.

Wide-eyed, Sophia listened to her husband, swamped under the weight of his enthusiasm. "Of course I shall stay with you, Heinrich," she said in answer to his question. "I will help you in every way I can."

CHAPTER 9

Could This *be Troy?*

HEINRICH STARTED the work at Hissarlik with eight men. Fortunately for Heinrich, he had hired a man as his overseer who soon proved to be reliable and competent. This man, Zaphyros Jannakis, a Greek, quickly won Heinrich's complete trust and confidence. His job was to pay out the wages to the workers, and he handled any bribes that became necessary to allow the work to progress. Many messy and troublesome matters were thus taken off Heinrich's mind, enabling him to concentrate more upon his digging. When Jannakis would come to Heinrich, telling of a bribe that had to be paid, or some other matter that could only be settled by payment, Heinrich would give him money from the belt of gold he carried around his waist, never questioning the honesty of Jannakis. And Jannakis did not fail him.

The digging went so smoothly and easily that he quickly enlarged his labor force to almost eighty workers in his eagerness to burrow into the soil and unearth the ruins he expected to find buried there. He was mistaken, however, to think he had the protection of the Turkish authorities.

They showed no trust or confidence in Heinrich's honesty. They made no allowances for the fact that he was spending freely and lavishly of his own money while they contributed nothing. It did not concern them that employment was being given to peasants who badly needed work. And all this was soon made very apparent to Heinrich.

Carefully and patiently, some workers eased out the loose soil while other spaded it into baskets and boxes and removed it where it would not hamper operations. Heinrich seemed to be everywhere at once, watching each spadeful of earth to see, as it was sifted into baskets, that no scrap of pottery or coins was missed by a careless worker. And where Heinrich was not, Sophia was, with equally eagle eye.

Then a stranger arrived on the scene, shortly after work began. The wily Safvet Pasha had posted this man as "observer." It did not take Heinrich long to understand that this individual was there as a spy for Safvet Pasha. He was to ensure that Heinrich would surrender any treasures he might discover. To Heinrich's great annoyance, this man stuck to him like a shadow. He followed his every movement. Whenever an opportunity arose, Sophia would turn all her charm upon this man in order to give Heinrich some freedom from his attentions. But no matter how cunning Heinrich tried to be, dodging about the site in an effort to tire the man out and lose him—the spy stuck close. The only relief Heinrich and Sophia had from this man's attentions was when they retired to the privacy of the small hut they had erected on the site. Even then, they were not sure he was not peeking from the dark outside into the lighted window.

"What are we to do, Sophia?" Heinrich asked. He wavered between anger and amusement. "I am determined that Safvet Pasha shall not get his hands on anything valuable we find."

Sophia thought for a moment. "Leave it to me, Heinrich," she said. "I will do my best to distract him and keep him occupied. But you will have to watch the workmen more closely while I watch him."

Never a patient man, Heinrich did his best to ignore the spy, but despite Sophia's efforts, arguments and quarrels were frequent and bitter. Sophia did her best, using all her great charm and beauty to engage the spy in conversation, and the man was susceptible to her charms. But he also feared the anger of Safvet Pasha, and Sophia was not always successful.

Impatience and frustration stirred Heinrich to violent activity. Bad weather had set in and the soil was turning into sticky mud. Disregarding rain and wind and storms, ignoring the bad cold he'd caught, Heinrich worked on. He was sure he had found the foundations of Priam's palace. Dressed masonry came to light, sometimes mixed with huge blocks of undressed stone. Old foundations had been built upon even older foundations. It was all ajumble, and Heinrich could make very little meaning of it. He was desperately anxious for acknowledgment from the world of archeology supporting the value of his work, and he made some wild guesses at what he had uncovered.

Even more immense walls were soon revealed from the

centuries of darkness. Surely, Heinrich thought, these must be the same walls the artist had drawn from Homer's description!

Then more burned debris appeared. In this, Heinrich found some coins, then bones and boar's teeth. Many stone spearheads came to light. He did not find any pottery. It began to seem like a rubbish heap.

Digging ever deeper, his excitement grew as small owllike terra-cotta figures appeared. More and more of them were found. Heinrich could not comprehend them. They must have some religious significance. But they seemed much too crude in workmanship to have been any part of the art work of Troy. "Perhaps," he said to Sophia, "they belonged to some barbarian people who occupied the ruins after Troy was destroyed?"

The work continued. Heinrich showed his finds to Frank Calvert, but Calvert could throw no light upon their meaning. Heinrich began to feel despondent. Was his dream of a lifetime only a fantasy after all?

Sophia did her best to keep him cheerful. Frank Calvert urged him to keep on and not be discouraged because these crude artifacts seemed too barbaric to have belonged to the Trojans. "It is possible," he suggested, "that they could date from a later, or even an earlier, period than Priam's Troy."

As he fingered the small objects, Heinrich grew more puzzled by their mystery. In appearance they seemed to belong more to the relics found in India than to anything Greek. At a 12-foot depth, stone knives, so sharp they could have been used as razors, were unearthed. Small clay boat-shaped things appeared. The purpose or use of such things was a mystery. Some of them had inscriptions that bore a resemblance to ancient Egyptian work.

Winter was approaching rapidly. Just as his men had cleared huge blocks of stone that had tumbled into an immense doorway, a violent storm broke over their heads. Heinrich realized that the work for that season must end. To continue was futile. The mud, the rain, the cold and bitter winds, were more than they could cope with. He paid off his workmen and, with Sophia, returned to Athens. They planned to spend the winter months sorting notes on their work, describing the objects that had been found, and trying to fathom their meaning and purpose.

When Heinrich's journal was sufficiently organized, he published it in a German periodical in several installments. He invited whatever comments and assistance other scholars could offer in his desire to understand the meaning of his finds.

Some scholars wrote articles saying he was mad. Many persisted in maintaining that Troy was nothing but an invention of the blind poet Homer. Others were convinced that Troy, if it existed at all, was to be found at Bunarbashi, not Hissarlik. Heinrich's evidence of the numerous springs at Bunarbashi, of the geographic accuracy of Homer and other ancient historians, availed him nothing against these critics. They dismissed such evidence as meaningless.

Heinrich was terribly angry. None of these smug

critics had spent a penny of his own visiting the site; none knew anything about the matter from personal observation.

The more Heinrich's efforts were rejected, the more determined he became to prove the correctness of his theory. Some correspondents were more kindly and encouraged Heinrich to go on with the excavations. Schröder's, the firm which had started Heinrich on his road to fame and fortune, presented him with a good deal of equipment, spades and wheelbarrows, to assist him in his labors.

Gratified to have had at least some recognition, he published his notes in book form, calling the book *Trojan Antiquities*.

In March, 1872, Heinrich and Sophia returned to Hissarlik. The weather stayed bad, so the couple spent the first few weeks preparing to start work. Heinrich had received much good advice urging him to take greater care than he had shown in order that he would not, unknowingly, damage buildings or relics beyond repair. He realized that his haste had damaged material that ought not to have been damaged, and he vowed to be more careful with his digging. He planned to keep more careful notes describing exactly what was found, where it was found, the time of finding, and the position of the object when it was found. His conscience bothered him for the stones already taken away from the site by the two Turks, but he was determined not to make such errors in the future.

Worried because nothing had been found of any consequence, by May, Heinrich knew moods of black despair. It was all Sophia could do to keep him from giving up his search. Then, a very strange thing happened.

There was a good deal of sickness in the area around Hissarlik, and there was little or no medical knowledge or help to combat it. The villagers bore their miseries as well as they could.

One day, a small girl came up to Heinrich. "The poor child," said the compassionate Sophia. "Heinrich, we must do something for her."

Heinrich studied the small girl. She was smothered with runny sores and her left eye was almost eaten away. She had a heavy cough. She was thin and undernourished, yet had managed to walk several miles to see if the "foreigners" at Hissarlik could help her.

Rightly or wrongly, Heinrich was always positive to the point of being obstinate. He had not forgotten his own sufferings when he was lost in the jungle of Panama. With a tenderness rare and unusual in him, except toward Sophia, he placed an arm upon the child's shoulders.

"Drink this," he commanded. The child swallowed a stiff dose of castor oil. And after they fed her, Heinrich took her aside. Standing before her he said, "You must practice these simple exercises like this, as often as you can. It will ease the pain in your chest and help your breathing. Your nasty cough should get better." Then he stretched his arms above his head, lowered them until they were horizontal with his shoulders, and then forward and down to his sides. He repeated it several times while the child copied him.

"Now," he said, "you must do one other thing if you want to get well. As often as you can, you must go down to the shore and bathe in the sea. You will find, child, it has a very great cleansing effect, for the waters of the sea contain many beneficial properties."

For the rest of his life, Heinrich marveled at the result of this encounter. A few weeks later, the girl returned to Heinrich's camp. Spotting Heinrich, she ran to him laughing. She dropped to her knees and kissed his hands. Faithfully, she had followed his advice, and instructions. The cough had largely disappeared. Although she had lost the sight of her left eye, her skin was now clean and clear, and she walked properly, instead of stumbling in pain.

May passed, and June followed. Small objects still emerged from the earth. Carefully, Heinrich recorded each find. He noted the depth of the find, its position and condition. This information would be vitally important in later reconstruction of the history of the site, what the buildings had been like and the purpose they had served. Heinrich began to understand the importance of proper labeling and recording as he studied his notes at the end of the day.

Summer progressed, and so did the work. Occasionally, Heinrich uncovered marble slabs with dedications inscribed upon them. These were carefully sketched and copied for later study. He found a group of jars huddled in soft earth and some delicate black pottery. This was more like the kind of artifact he was expecting of the Trojan civilization.

"But Sophia," he confessed sadly one day, "we really have discovered little proof of King Priam or Paris and Helen."

Hope revived and excitement flared anew toward the end of June. Heinrich found a small but beautifully executed bas-relief showing Apollo and the four horses of the sun. It was an exquisite carving, showing a high degree of skill. Obviously, this was the work of a master sculptor.

But the brief surge of excitement waned as summer's heat grew. Scorpions and noxious insects swarmed in the diggings. Hot winds and dust storms swept over them as they tried to work.

Heinrich was discouraged. He complained to Sophia that he did not feel well.

Sophia felt his forehead. "Heinrich, you have a fever," she said. "I think we should stop work now. It is best to wait until the weather is more suitable."

"I suppose you are right, my dear," he said despondently. "But let us keep going just a little longer."

Reluctantly, Sophia agreed.

In August, with most of the workmen already paid off, Heinrich was scratching about in one of the trenches. The observer of Safvet Pasha, tired of the long months without sign of treasure, spent much of his time dozing in the sun.

Suddenly, Heinrich called guardedly to Sophia from the trench.

"Look," he cried, "here is something of interest at last!" He pointed to a skeleton he had uncovered. "I'm

Heinrich believed the ancient legends.

sure it must be the bones of a woman," he said. "Look how small they are. She seems to have died in a fire. Could she, perhaps, have died in the destruction of Troy?" Desperately, he wished to believe it true.

"I am sure you must be right—that she is a woman," Sophia said. In her hand she held three beautiful gold earrings and a gold brooch. Heinrich had found them beside the skeleton.

At last, Heinrich thought, we are on the right track, and this new evidence fired his enthusiasm all over again. But his fever, the weather, and the clouds of dust got the better of his determination. The rains came, and they watched the dusty plain turn into a sea of mud. Work had to be abandoned.

Sophia, too, now had feverish attacks, yet they were pleased with the meager results of the season's digging.

Once back in Athens, they soon recovered from the fever. Heinrich made a hurried trip back to Hissarlik, where he took some photographs of the site. He hoped they would prove helpful in enabling him to reconstruct what the place had looked like.

The scholar, who had lain dormant in Heinrich for most of his life, now took complete command of him. He did not neglect his business interests, but their intrusion upon his search for Troy became a source of annoyance. His archeological instinct had been sharpened by his experiences in the field, and his life now became dedicated utterly to archeology.

Sensing scholarly success within his grasp, as once he had foretold financial success, Heinrich did not waste the winter months in Athens. Mycenae had begun to intrigue him. The city to which Agamemnon had returned from the burning of Troy, only to be murdered cruelly upon his arrival, furnished another link in the chain that would prove the truth of Troy.

Heinrich wrote to the Greek government, asking permission to excavate at Mycenae. He offered to build a museum with his own funds, which he would give to Greece, and anything of value or importance that was found would be housed in this museum. He reminded them of the glory of their past and pointed out the great value of such a museum to Greece. All he asked in return was that the museum should bear his name. Surely a reasonably vanity?

Curtly, and unkindly, his offer was refused.

"Those fools!" Heinrich raved to Sophia when he learned of the refusal. "What right have they to stand in the way of science? Do I ask any help or any money from them? Petty officials, they are the plague of the earth!"

Gently, Sophia urged him to be patient. "Soon," she said, "it will be time to return to Troy. Who knows what we may find?"

Fortunately for Heinrich, Troy still held him fast in the grip of its mystery, and he did not long brood over the churlish attitude of the Greek government.

CHAPTER 10

The Treasure Is Found

WHEN THEY RETURNED to Hissarlik, Heinrich and Sophia were immediately swamped with fresh intrigue and pettiness.

"Sophia," Heinrich cried, returning from an examination of the site, "the watchman we left in charge has been selling stones from the walls! What shall we do?"

"Selling stones?" said Sophia, aghast. "Whatever for?"

"The villagers round about have been buying them, breaking them up, and using them to repair their huts! Will there be no end to this mischief?"

Angrily, as soon as he could find the watchman, Heinrich fired him. Then he hired another man and armed him with a gun to ward off any peasant caught trying to steal the ancient masonry. Heinrich also complained to Safvet Pasha. Far from giving any sympathy to the complaint, Safvet Pasha replied that the permit was withdrawn. He accused Heinrich of taking out of the country all the treasure he had found.

"But, Sophia," he cried, "there hasn't been any treasure! Is the man mad?"

They decided to go ahead for as long as they could, ignoring Safvet Pasha. Work commenced once again. But their troubles were not yet over. The winds whistled through the boards of the hut, and one night, while Sophia and Heinrich were sleeping, the draft blew a spark from the fireplace and soon one whole wall of the wooden hut was aflame. Heinrich awoke to find the room full of smoke. Hastily he aroused Sophia.

"Quick, Sophia!" he called. "Carry out all the journals and records. Take them safely away from the fire!"

More asleep than awake, Sophia roused and threw on a robe. She gathered up armfuls of notes and books and ran outside. She set them on the ground and returned, again and again, until all were safe. Then she joined Heinrich, throwing great shovelfuls of damp earth over the blaze. Their efforts were successful and they subdued the blaze. Relaxing and recovering from their labors, they gazed at each other across the room. Heinrich gave voice to the doubt both wondered.

"Are the beloved ghosts of Troy conspiring to prevent me from disturbing their sleep of centuries?"

"No," said Sophia quietly. "You seek to honor them, Heinrich, not do them harm."

"I don't know, Sophia. Perhaps they prefer to remain buried with the rubble of their glory. Perhaps they do not want their tragic ending once more revealed to the daylight." Heinrich shook his head in puzzlement.

As bright day dawned, the dark mood vanished. They had some of the workmen repair the wall and once more the hut was snug.

Having decided to defy Safvet Pasha, Heinrich knew he must work fast. He had to accomplish as much as possible before they tried to stop him. In some strange fashion, since the fire and his deep gloom, Heinrich seemed to know that something important was about to happen.

In April, the first clue came. The men began to uncover and remove earth from some stones. As they worked, Heinrich skipping about watching every shovel, the street of an ancient city emerged. Carefully tracing its outline, clearing earth and rubbish, they followed along the street. Nine great clay jars, six feet tall, were brushed clear of earth as they were revealed. There they stood, in exactly the position in which they had been buried. Jars of this kind had never been found before. As they continued to clear away earth, Heinrich examined the position of some stones and discovered them to be parts of two great stone gateways. He felt sure, now, he was at the gates of Troy. Then emerged more clay vases and broken rubble. A beautiful silver vase was found next, and inside it a silver beaker.

Determined to outwit Safvet Pasha's spy, Heinrich hastily split the workmen into smaller groups and put them to work in widely separated corners of the trenches.

"Now," he said to Sophia, "let him keep his eyes on all of them!"

The poor spy ran about the excavations trying desperately to watch everywhere and everything at once, while Heinrich and Sophia grinned at each other. Heinrich was absolutely certain that something important was about to happen.   (Heinrich, determined to keep his finds from the greedy Pasha, never did give the exact date on which his great find was made.   It has been pieced together since, and is probably, as close as we can judge, approximately the end of May.)

About the thirtieth of May, 1873, the workmen were digging a small trench below what Heinrich believed to be the outer wall of Priam's palace.

Quivering with excitement, certain that his nose smelled treasure, Heinrich scrambled about the excavation.   Kneeling in the earth beside the stone structure he had named the *Scaean* (western) Gate, Heinrich saw something gleam.   By great good fortune, the two men with him had not noticed the gleam.

Clambering up out of the trench, he ordered the two men to stop work.

"Line up," Heinrich ordered, "and collect your day's pay!"

Casting bewildered glances at each other, the men shrugged, dropped their tools and strode to the pay table.

"Sophia," Heinrich called, "come here, quickly!"

"What is it?" she asked, as she ran up to her husband.

"Quick," Heinrich whispered, "pay off the men.   Tell them it's my birthday!   Tell them anything you like, but send them away.   All of them!   As quickly as you can!"

Not pausing to question further, Sophia ran to the nearest group of workmen.   "Everybody is to come to the table and collect their pay.   It is Dr. Schliemann's birthday, but he forgot it until just now. It is a holiday, but you will be paid anyway."

As soon as possible, Sophia returned to Heinrich in the trench. "They are gone, Heinrich. They are laughing and singing at the unexpected holiday, but Safvet Pasha's man is very curious. I think he has decided to follow the men and find out what is happening."

"Look, Sophia! *Look here!*"

Sophia knelt down in the trench where Heinrich pointed to an object. They were at a depth of almost 30 feet, below the wall. They saw a copper container about 18 inches high by 36 inches long. A closer look told them the container was broken. Peering through the broken side, they saw gleaming silver objects. On top of the container were two objects that looked like helmets. On top of these there was a five-foot depth of burned rubble packed so hard it felt like stone. The huge walls had been built on top of this hard-packed, burned rubble.

Heinrich scrambled to the top of the trench and peered around. Then, rubbing his hands with satisfaction, he climbed back down to Sophia. "It's as I thought," he said. "The spy didn't know I was here. He's following the workmen home. Well, he won't find out much! Quickly now, Sophia, run and fetch your big red shawl. Try not to let anyone see you. Get back as fast as you can!"

As soon as Sophia returned with the shawl, they pried open the copper container and began to lift out the gleaming objects. When they had them all out, they wrapped the shawl over the top and, with the heavy bundle, like two thieves in the night, they scuttled back to their hut. Safely inside, they locked the door, breathing hard from their efforts. Then they sat looking at the large bundle on the wooden table.

Sophia turned back the corners of the red shawl until it hung over the edges of the table. Together they stood in awe, gazing wordlessly at the lovely objects the earth had yielded up to them.

"Heinrich," Sophia gasped. "It's incredible!"

"I swear, Sophia," Heinrich said, "the Turks will never get their hands on this beauty. They'd as soon melt it down for precious metal—sooner—than house it in a museum. It will mean nothing to them!"

"Surely, this is the most fantastic quantity of ancient treasure that has ever been found," Sophia said.

And, indeed, it was.

The treasure, originally, had been carefully stored. Bigger pieces had smaller treasures inside them. Sophia and Heinrich began to spread the treasures over the table; a gold bottle and two gold cups. Next they set aside a copper shield and a large copper pot. There was a silver vase and a similar one made of copper. There was an amber cup. There were three big silver vases. In the biggest of these they found two gold diadems, a smaller gold headband, four gold ear pendants, fifty-six gold earrings, and nearly nine thousand gold rings and buttons. There was a big silver goblet, six silver knife blades, and more than a dozen copper spearheads!

Sophia and Heinrich sucked in their breath, hardly

daring to believe what their eyes showed them. Heinrich picked up one of the diadems. It was fantastic. The elaborate beauty consisted of nearly a hundred gold chains which formed a headdress with floral pendants and tassels hanging from the sides. Such a thing had never been seen before, or found anywhere. Diadems were usually simple jeweled bands worn around the head. This beautiful headdress must surely be Trojan!

Laughing like a delighted schoolboy, Heinrich held up golden objects and watched them shimmer. Then he placed the beautiful headdress upon Sophia's dark hair, completing the work with rings and other treasures. He stood back to look at the effect and silently, he regarded his beloved Sophia.

Heinrich Schliemann remained silent for several minutes, then tears came into his eyes and trickled down his face. "Sophia," he whispered huskily, "the beautiful Helen of Troy could not have been more lovely. Now I know why Paris fell so in love with her he carried her off. Was the destruction of Troy too high a price to pay for Helen? I confess, my dear, I could not say as I gaze at your loveliness."

After they had become calmer, Heinrich and Sophia fingered the other objects of their find. There were some small ivory carvings, a lead figurine, and other trinkets. Heinrich was convinced this was Priam's treasure.

"Now let them say that Troy is a myth," he said boldly. Yet he was a little puzzled. Some of the objects showed a well-developed skill of workmanship and others were obviously the work of crude craftsmen. What was it all

Heinrich regarded his beloved Sophia.

doing jumbled up and buried together? Well, that mystery would have to wait for a later time. The immediate problem was how to get the treasure safely away before Safvet Pasha's spy discovered what they had found.

"I am sure," Heinrich said, "he already suspects something. He'll be back snooping around our hut."

Heinrich was right. The spy arrived and banged on the door. He demanded that he be allowed to search the house and examine all the boxes Heinrich used for packing objects recovered from the rubble of the mound.

Angrily, Heinrich sent him away, refusing to allow him into the house. "Come back tomorrow," he said. "Then you can search as you will. Today is a holiday and I do not wish to be disturbed."

Whining and grumbling of the anger of his master, Safvet Pasha, the spy went away.

Carefully and tenderly, Heinrich and Sophia packed the golden treasure in straw and then into half a dozen baskets and a large sack. They waited until it was very dark. Then, cautiously and carefully, trying not to make a sound, they slipped away from the hut. Both knew the spy might be awake, watching their door, or sleeping lightly on the ground outside. It was a risk that had to be taken, but they succeeded. Soon, they reached Frank Calvert's house and left the packages with him. From there, the treasures were to be quietly—and, they hoped, without arousing suspicion—shipped to Heinrich's home in Athens.

Before dawn broke, Heinrich and Sophia had slipped back into the hut.

Next day, willingly, Heinrich allowed the spy to examine all the boxes of pottery and clay figurines stored in the room. Nonchalantly, he and Sophia made cursory examinations of the trenches and watched the workmen at their tasks. .

Frank Calvert succeeded in shipping the packages as Heinrich directed. Probably he did not know, or did not wish to be told, what the packages contained. When news of the safe shipment reached Heinrich, he abruptly called a halt to all work and paid off the men. Heinrich made known that he was disgusted beyond endurance by the attitude of the Turkish authorities and that he would never return to Troy. "They have harassed and beset my efforts to serve science and knowledge, every step of the way," he complained.

Then Sophia and Heinrich returned to Athens.

When they were settled down in their house, Sophia and Heinrich wrote a careful and detailed description of each of the treasures they had found. When all had been catalogued and described, they began to think about hiding the treasure. Heinrich knew perfectly well that once news of his find was out, there would be an uproar. So they carefully repacked each item, and then, with the aid of Sophia's family, placed each package back into the earth from which it came, each buried in a different place.

"Now," Heinrich said, once more rubbing his hands

with glee, "I am ready for them! Now let them find it!"

As soon as Heinrich published the description of his find at Troy, the uproar he expected broke over his head. The Turkish authorities accused him of stealing treasure belonging to them. Heinrich countered by reminding them of their broken promises. He reminded them of the officials who had stood in his way, interfering with every part of the work. "It is you," he thundered, "who have broken promises, not I. What help or interest in my work did you give me?"

The bitter quarrel lasted for several years. It passed in and out of many courts, but nothing could be done because Heinrich kept the treasure safely hidden and many people simply did not believe his story. Others decided he could not possibly have made up such detailed descriptions of the treasures he described.

There were also those whose interest and enthusiasm were aroused by the reports of Heinrich's work. His unorthodox methods did not raise eyebrows in England. The English had a long history of eccentric characters, many of whom had helped England to her greatness. Prime Minister Gladstone was very interested in Heinrich's find, and Queen Victoria, too, expressed her pleasure at the discovery.

Heinrich knew very well that sooner or later he would have to offer his treasure to some powerful government, together with a suitable offer to provide a building to house the golden objects, but he could not make up his mind to whom it should go. The Turks were still trying to force him to return it to them. England and America had always treated him kindly and well, and he felt affection for both countries, but he could not decide. Greece was too weak to stand up to Turkey if he gave it to Greece. And always there was the challenge to triumph over those critics in France and Germany who mocked and ridiculed him and would not acknowledge the scholarship he so wished to have recognized.

Some of Heinrich's German critics were so arrogantly sure he was bluffing they openly demanded he produce his evidence so they could examine it themselves. There were hints that he had acted like a common thief. "Gold seeker!" he was called. "Treasure hunter!" others said. All of them ignored the fact that Heinrich Schliemann was a millionaire many times over and that if he found treasure it was by his own efforts, paid for with his own money—and that he did not need gold. They forgot that they had ridiculed him for even digging at Hissarlik, because, they said, Troy was at Bunarbashi. And why, if Heinrich was interested only in finding treasure, did he announce his finds, instead of keeping it all to himself?

Finding no chinks in the armor of disdain with which the French and German scholars shielded themselves from him, Heinrich and Sophia went to England. In London they talked of the discovery with Gladstone, and the Queen received them. Gladstone was very interested in Heinrich's theories of Troy.

Heinrich and Sophia gave lectures, Sophia sharing the platform with her husband. Her beauty and perfect English captivated her audiences. Those who listened to this trim and delicate creature found it hard to picture her grubbing about the excavations of Troy. Yet her conviction, her sincerity and authority, were such that none disbelieved their adventures.

At one of their lectures, unknown to Heinrich and Sophia, a young man sat listening with rapt attention. This young man was Arthur Evans, still a schoolboy. In later years he set the crown of fame securely upon the head of Heinrich Schliemann. He was to enlarge the picture and give meaning to Heinrich's discoveries that are of immense value to the whole world.

Pleased beyond measure by their gratifying experiences in England, Heinrich and Sophia returned to Athens.

But the treasure remained buried.

CHAPTER 11

Golden Mycenae

HEINRICH WORRIED CONSTANTLY about the treasure of Troy. He wanted it properly housed and on display where others could enjoy and marvel at it. Mostly, he wanted to silence the critics who stoutly maintained there was no treasure. His bitter legal fight with the Turkish authorities over the ownership of the treasure had now moved into the law courts of Greece.

Not the least of Heinrich's reasons for wanting the treasure safe in a museum was the fact that another project occupied his mind and he was anxious to get it under way. For this project, Heinrich knew only too well that he would need the cooperation, good will and support of the Greek government.

When he did not receive such encouragement, he went directly to the king.

Despondently, he talked the matter over with Sophia. "Neither the king nor the government seem to be interested," Heinrich explained. "I offer to build a museum for them from my own pocket. They would have the treasures for always, to bring visitors and scholars

139

from all over the world. What more do they want?"

"It is politics," Sophia said. "The times are uneasy.
Turkey is strong, but Greece is weak. Besides, you are
still fighting in the courts here over the treasure and nobody knows what the outcome may be."

This made Heinrich pause. Suppose the courts ordered him to give the Trojan treasure to Turkey? Something had to be done about it, and at once.

"I know what we will do," he said. "Let us get the
treasure to England and put it on exhibition there. We
are liked in England and we can trust them. The treasure will be safe, and England, certainly, has nothing to
fear and will not be intimidated by Turkey."

Some months passed, then they moved the treasure to
England, and as soon as it was on exhibition, some of
the furor died down. Those who had questioned the
very existence of the treasure were silenced. Many
papers were published in which scholars speculated on
the people who had buried it at Troy so many centuries
before. Very few accepted Heinrich's belief that it represented the treasure of King Priam, buried before Troy
was destroyed. But they were all theories.

The young Arthur Evans, who had listened so atten-
tively to Heinrich's lectures, was especially interested in
the exhibition and he spent many hours studying the
beautiful gold and silver objects.

While Heinrich was trying to obtain permission from
the Greeks for a new excavation, he was approached again
by the Turks. Proof of the treasure could not now be
denied. Perhaps they hoped to lure him back to arrest
him. Or it may have been that since Heinrich spent

lavishly on his digging, if they got him to work at Troy again he might find more treasure and this time they would make sure they seized it all. They renewed Heinrich's permit to dig at Troy. They assured him full use of the land. They did *not* offer him any financial assistance, but they agreed to a fifty-fifty split of any treasure that was found.

In their eagerness, the Turks quickly settled their quarrel with Heinrich in the Greek courts. They accepted his offer of compensation, fifty thousand francs. It was a trifling sum compared to the priceless treasure of Troy, and Heinrich gleefully paid it. The settlement lifted a great load of worry from his shoulders.

"Now," he said to Sophia, "we need not concern ourselves with the treasure. It is safe for all time. Sometime soon, I will arrange a permanent home for it. But that can wait."

"And will you go back to Troy now?" Sophia asked.

"No," Heinrich replied. "I have another plan. We have done our work at Troy. Let them say what they will, we have proved the truth of Homer. We have proved Troy was real. Let them argue. I plan now to give them more proof. It is to Mycenae that we shall go. And there's another thing. The Turks have been allowing all kinds of people to tear at the site of Troy, so heaven alone knows what kind of mess they have made there!"

Heinrich was now a confirmed and dedicated archeologist. Mycenae had long drawn him to its ruins, and to prepare for excavations there, Heinrich turned to Pausanias to guide him in his search.

Pausanias, a writer of the second century A.D., had visited Mycenae and described the city as it looked then, long after its glory had vanished. Pausanias wrote:

In the ruins of Mycenae is a fountain called Perseia and the underground buildings of Atreus and his sons, where their treasure is buried. There is the tomb of Atreus and there are also the tombs of Agamemnon and his charioteer whom Aegisthus murdered on their return from Troy. These tombs are within the walls. A little outside the walls are the tombs of Clytemnestra and Aegisthus for they were considered unworthy to lie in the same hallowed ground with Agamemnon and those murdered with him.

Heinrich could see no reason for not taking Pausanias at his word, and he pondered the description given by the ancient author. Some scholars believed that Pausanias referred to the walls of the city of Mycenae when he mentioned tombs *inside* and *outside* the walls. Heinrich disagreed. He reasoned that when Pausanias visited Mycenae, the city walls were already a tumbled ruin. These ruins could still be traced without much difficulty. Heinrich believed Pausanias meant that the tomb of Agamemnon was to be found inside the walls of the Acropolis, and that Clytemnestra and Aegisthus were buried outside this building. Heinrich knew very well that the Acropolis usually stood on the highest part of a city and was the center for any important event that took place. Lesser buildings, temples and tombs, were usually clustered around it.

The more Heinrich studied, the more enthusiastic he became, and he recalled having seen the wonderful Lion Gate at Mycenae, which still stood above the earth, and he felt very sure that somewhere in its vicinity he could find the tombs of Agamemnon and his family.

Agamemnon, one of the Achaean kings, had returned home with captives and booty, his share of the loot from Troy. His triumph was short-lived. His queen, Clytemnestra, fearful of her fate when her husband discovered her infidelity during his absence, plotted with her lover to kill Agamemnon. At the banquet celebrating the victorious home-coming, Clytemnestra and her lover, Aegisthus, murdered Agamemnon and his charioteer.

Heinrich believed the truth of this story as firmly as he had believed in the destruction and existence of Troy.

The attitude of the Greek government softened, perhaps because Heinrich had settled his quarrel with the Turks. There could be no denying that Heinrich was a world-famous figure with such powerful influence that he could go over the heads of the officials of any government to king or president. The Greeks gave in to his steady pressure and granted him permission to excavate at Mycenae.

Delightedly, Heinrich made his plans and assembled his equipment.

With light hearts and high spirits, Heinrich and Sophia reached Mycenae. Then Heinrich exploded! The Greeks, too, had set a man to watch over his activity and report any treasure found and any suspicious movements made!

Angrily, Heinrich fired off protests to Athens. It did no good.

"Are we to go through this all again?" he said wearily to Sophia.

It was very vexing. The official spy was constantly under his feet poking his nose into every nook and cranny as Heinrich explored. Bitter quarrels went on all the time and Heinrich kept up a steady stream of protesting telegrams to Athens. Word of the difficulties spread through Europe and once more, like angry bees, the armchair critics buzzed about Heinrich's head.

The Greek official, in turn, protested to his superiors that Heinrich was hampering *him* in *his* duty! He complained that Heinrich was wantonly tearing down walls and relics of the glory of ancient Greece and Rome.

Heinrich brushed the protest aside. He was seeking a civilization that was long dead before Greece, to which it gave birth, had risen. There were countless details known of Greece and Rome and no shortage of relics for students to study. But who had found Troy? Who had proved the truth of Homer? Greece and Rome were almost contemporary, when compared to the people Heinrich was seeking.

It did not matter to the critics of his exploits that Heinrich was paying for his excavations, enriching science and knowledge from his own pocket; not one penny of outside money was given to him for his work. They ridiculed his archeology. They called him a "treasure seeker" and pointed to his adventure in California as proof. He lusted after gold, they said. And that was *all* he was interested in. The proof of the theories he offered from Troy was still ignored. That his own developing skill and under-

standing of good archeological practice, his faith and
tenacity, had won out against all who tried to stop him
from finding Troy, was not allowed to become a factor
on the credit side of the ledger.

With bitterness in his heart, but with his beloved
Sophia to soften the blows and urge him on, Heinrich
continued to work. He did his best to be careful of
Greek and Roman relics. But when they stood upon
older structures he wished to examine and reveal, he tore
them down. All the ridicule had no power to shake his
faith in ancient historians, and once more he preferred
their guidance to that of men who had not made the
slightest effort to go into the field and study the evidence
at first hand.

Remembering that he had found the treasure of Troy
close beside the main city gate, Heinrich decided to begin
digging beside the famous Lion Gate.

In August, 1876, Heinrich and Sophia, with sixty
workers, commenced digging. Eagerly, the Greek official
looked over their shoulders. But little of any note was
found. The now familiar debris revealed combs and
needles, some vases and goblets, clay animals and figurines
and buttons. Then, early in September, they found two
tombstones.

The heat and dust, the hard work, were beginning to
affect Heinrich's health. Being watched like a thief
played havoc with his nerves and his temper was short,
so the discovery of the tombstones gave him a welcome
incentive to continue his excavations.

The next few days' digging revealed more broken

tombstones and a gold button. Heinrich believed he was
on the right trail, and he was intrigued by the circle of
stone seats, like a small arena, which was now revealed.
While he pondered the purpose and meaning of the circle of seats, Heinrich set the men digging about the remains of a large house.

Upon reflection, Heinrich remembered how Euripides
had mentioned the people of Mycenae being called to
the agora to see the lamb with the golden fleece. The
agora served many purposes, and all important announce-
ments were made from the center of a circle of seats. He
remembered, too, that other ancient writers and ob-

View of Mycenae.

servers had described how heroes were buried *within* the agora. Heinrich felt very sure the circle represented the agora. What he sought would be found within that circle!

Summer was over. Heavy rains beat down, turning the dust to mud again. Eagerly, Heinrich worked on.

A fascinating vase was discovered in the house where he insisted on working, and it told much of the people who had lived at Mycenae. This painted vase showed warriors marching off to battle. Their helmets and armor matched others found in ancient Egyptian ruins worn by a strange people whom the Egyptians described as "people

Lion Gate.

from the lands of the sea." The vase furnished an important clue to the civilization Heinrich was bringing back to life.

In October, while digging deep into the floor of the agora, Heinrich discovered a large rock tomb, twenty feet long and half as wide. He found nothing except some gold buttons and a few ivory objects, so he came to the conclusion that robbers had long ago plundered the tomb.

Then, Heinrich moved farther toward the center of the circle. When he was 15 feet deep, his spade struck a thick layer of pebbles. Instantly, he was alert. Carefully removing the layer of pebbles, he found three bodies. They were covered with clay and what appeared to be the remains of a funeral pyre. He called Sophia to come quickly to his side, *for he had seen the gleam of gold on one of the bodies!*

Heinrich was too excited to work himself, so Sophia slid down into the narrow opening and, with a small knife, carefully and laboriously she scraped away the clay from the bodies.

Once more, Heinrich's faith in the truth of ancient writers and heroes was triumphantly justified. An incredible treasure was soon revealed. There were fifteen gold diadems, fourteen gold crosses of laurel leaves, and a silver cup. Fragments of painted vases were found, with many more obsidian knives.

Moisture and exposure to the air soon did their work, and the skeletons crumbled away, but the treasure was real enough. Heinrich noted that the design and construction of these ornaments was much simpler than the elegant treasures he found at Troy. He did not know why, but had not time to analyze the puzzle—he continued to dig.

At a fresh spot within the circle of the agora, he found another grave. It contained only a few obsidian knives. It was strange, he thought, but with determination, he dug lower than the 9-foot depth of this grave.

Triumph was sweet to Heinrich. *A little below the first grave, he found a chamber containing three bodies and the most incredible treasure of the past ever discovered!*

The workmen had been dismissed, but soldiers guarded the site. The authorities were only too painfully aware of the troubles that followed Heinrich's discovery of treasure at Troy. By hastily placing the soldiers on guard at the site, they were able to prevent any repetition of that sorry episode. And so long as they did not interfere with the work, Heinrich had no objection to this action.

Once again, Sophia scrambled into the narrow opening, carefully scraped away the clay, and gingerly handed out the treasure.

Into Heinrich's trembling hands she passed a dagger; a gold crown of shimmering, delicate leaves; two scepters of gold plated on silver. There were eight diadems and six double crosses. Gold necklaces followed, then a gold flower on a silver stem. There were gold goblets and vases, and wine jars with gold lids hinged with fine gold wire. Almost a thousand thin pieces of gold, shaped like leaves, stars, insects, and other creatures were found in the tomb. Many gold plaques with decorations delicately etched upon them completed the fantastic treasure.

Feverish with excitement, Heinrich set to work again as soon as the treasure was safely out of the way. He chose a place west of the great find because he had noticed the soil in this place seemed different, darker than the rest of the circle.

For 15 feet he found nothing but broken pottery. At 24 feet he came upon a circular stone object which he believed to be an altar. This stone object had a hole at the top, and Heinrich believed this was for offerings to the dead buried below. He was right.

A few feet beneath the altar, Heinrich found another tomb. *The five bodies within were covered with gold and jewels.* Gold death masks covered the faces of the bodies. The masks were stylized, but the features were clear enough to give a good idea of the people they represented, what they looked like, and, perhaps, clues to character. Each mask bore different features and there was a wide range of character between the etched faces. This treasure house of the past yielded up gold breastplates, a gold crown of leaves, and eleven huge gold goblets.

One special goblet greatly excited Heinrich. He believed he had found the "cup of Nestor." This, surely, was proof and justification. The cup *must* have been Nestor's! Heinrich was led astray by his eagerness. Although this cup *did* almost exactly fit the description of it in the *Iliad,* there was a big difference. In the eleventh book of the *Iliad,* Homer says that Nestor's cup had *four* handles. The cup found by Heinrich had only *two*

Objects found at Mycenae.

handles.   Nevertheless, Heinrich was not disturbed by such a minor discrepancy.   Two handles or four—the cup was close enough to Homer's description to give added strength to the truthful observance and reporting of the ancient poet.

The rest of the treasure from this grave consisted of gold belts and brooches; four hundred pieces of gold that were thought to be coins; small gold ornamental axes, gold pins, huge gold buttons, and one hundred and fifty of the odd-shaped gold disks.   There were also gold plates, bronze rapiers, copper caldrons, gold ornaments of all kinds, and a large cow's head, a religious symbol, made of silver with gold horns.

Excitement ran high as Heinrich neared completion of the excavation of the agora.

Heinrich found another grave containing a body, but the body disintegrated to dust almost immediately.   In this grave Heinrich found a gold diadem, a gold drinking cup, and a few stone and clay ornaments.

Envious commentators remarked that Heinrich Schliemann had a sixth sense for finding gold.   They said Heinrich had an instinct like that of a water diviner.   True enough, he did have an unerring instinct of the right places to dig for the past, but his gift and his skill were based upon more than instinct.   He believed, simply, in the veracity of the ancient writers.   He followed directions they supplied.   Others failed because they chose their own cleverness before the truth of the ancients.

One more triumph came to Heinrich before he left

Mycenae—for Heinrich, the most satisfying of all.

He had returned to work on the first grave shaft. His first examination had revealed nothing there. Now, poking about inside again, he found something he had missed the first time—three more bodies. There was not much treasure except some gold armor and leaves spread over a body. The two gold masks were the most exciting. One of them, Heinrich was convinced, was the death mask of Agamemnon. Heinrich lifted the gold mask from the face and kissed it.

Realizing the incredible luck of his find, he hurriedly sent for a painter to record the features of the face under the mask. Trembling with fear lest the face crumble to dust, he waited impatiently for the painter to arrive. Finally a druggist arrived and succeeded in covering the body with preservative. Afterwards it was taken to Athens.

Heinrich's work at Mycenae was done. With Sophia, he returned to his house in Athens, to prepare the notes of his discoveries for publication.

Heinrich was not at all disturbed by the presence of what he thought to be the body of Cassandra, a Trojan, buried with Greeks. Pausanias had described as much and Heinrich believed him. After Agamemnon carried Cassandra off from Troy, he made her his slave and mistress; thus she came to be buried at Mycenae.

Heinrich wanted the whole world to share his great triumph, and he reported upon his work to the King of Greece:

With extreme joy I announce to Your Majesty that I have discovered the tombs which tradition, echoed by Pausanias, has designated as the sepulchres of Agamemnon, Cassandra, Euryme-don and their companions who were killed by Clytemnestra and her lover Aegisthus. They were surrounded by a double circle of stone slabs which would not have been erected unless they were great personages. In the tombs I found immense treasures of the most ancient objects of pure gold.

These treasures alone will fill a great museum, the most wonderful in the world, and for centuries to come thousands of foreigners will flock to Greece to see them. I work only for the pure love of science, and accordingly I have no claim on these treasures. I give them intact and with lively enthusiasm to Greece. God grant that these treasures may become the cornerstone of an immense national wealth.

In happy anticipation, Heinrich awaited a reply from the King. Surely now he would be honored. This gesture must bring its reward. The seal of good scholarship would be firmly set upon his work and his services to science.

At fifty-four years of age, Heinrich Schliemann trembled with delight at the prospect of acceptance from the scholastic world.

The letter came. Excitedly, Heinrich tore open the envelope, then let the sheet of paper fall to the table.

"What is it?" Sophia asked anxiously.

Heinrich passed the sheet to his wife, and Sophia hurriedly read the few lines of writing. It was a terse note of thanks!

"What do they want of me!" Heinrich burst out. "They give me free advice. They say 'do this, don't do that.' 'Dig here, not there.' They criticize my efforts in every way. They grant me neither skill nor knowledge. None of them has offered me a penny to help pay for the work. None of them has offered to work for me or with me. And *this!*" He snatched up the note. "I give them an immense treasure, asking nothing for myself. I give them a building to house it and this. . . . They might as well be honest and say, 'Thank you Heinrich Schliemann. You may come again and spend your own money digging treasure. Just as long as we get the treasures!'"

Sophia stood up and walked behind her husband's chair. "Do not fret too much, Heinrich. It is shabby treatment I know, and I know how it hurts you. But try to remember, the future will decide the values of this. The future will know whom to honor. They cannot take away the truth of your accomplishments."

CHAPTER 12

A Slip of Paper

FOR ALMOST TWO YEARS Heinrich relaxed and rested from his labors. He built himself a house in Athens, modeling it along classic Greek lines, using great quantities of marble in its construction. He filled it with the antiquities he had collected throughout his life.

When the house was finished, Heinrich settled in with Sophia. Even in this commonplace action, his enemies found cause for sport. They made cutting remarks about Heinrich's house being pretentious, calling it a cold tomb, a marble mausoleum. Heinrich was too busy and too happy to pay heed. He liked the house and so did Sophia. That was enough for them.

This spell of domestic bliss did much to soothe Heinrich. Where Catherine Lyschin had kept his children from him, preventing any warmth from growing between them and their father, Sophia encouraged Heinrich in his love of his Greek children. Heinrich had been away often, but he hardly realized how much he had missed them.

156

He spent many happy hours with his daughter Androm-
ache and his son Agamemnon.   He told them of the
origins of their names, filled their young minds with
stories of the glorious past of Greece, their native land.
He encouraged them to study, to learn all they could
about the peoples who gave the world so much civilization.   It was, indeed, a wonderfully happy time for Heinrich, and for Sophia and the children.   Others might think
the house in Athens was a cold tomb, but they did not
know the love and warmth of the family there who made
it a cozy and pleasant place to be.

In a brief span of eight weeks, Heinrich wrote a book
in both French and German.   He described his archeological work and his discoveries, offered theories of the origin
and meaning of the artifacts he had found.   Prime
Minister Gladstone, in England, wrote a forty-page introduction to the book.   But Heinrich was laughed at in
France and Germany.

After giving many more talks and lectures with Sophia
all over Europe, Heinrich grew restless again.   There
were far more ancient cities still buried in the ground
than he had dug up.   He was anxious to get back to work,
still craving for acceptance by those who mocked him and
refused to take him seriously.   Once again, he became a
wanderer over the face of the earth, searching for its hidden past.

Heinrich Schliemann made several more forays to
Troy.   On one of the earliest he found another small

treasure, consisting of gold and silver rings and bracelets, gold beads and small bars of gold. The Turkish authorities took two thirds of the treasure and Heinrich was allowed to keep the rest. He added it to his collection in the great house in Athens, where it rested in splendor, watched over by a large bust of Homer.

It is sad that Heinrich Schliemann was mostly wrong in the periods and dates he ascribed to his discoveries. But his errors were honest, and from his discoveries came the true picture. Heinrich believed he had unearthed a vast civilization which had covered the entire eastern Mediterranean. He thought it was probably Egyptian or African in origin.

Heinrich decided to dig at Tiryns. Many of his guides and friends told him there was nothing to be found there, and archeologists maintained that ruins existing at the site were only medieval. Heinrich paid no attention. He trusted Homer. Also, Pausanias had described the vast walls of Tiryns, supposed to be the birthplace of Heracles, as being comparable to the pyramids because they were so huge.

Heinrich began to dig, and the familiar pattern again emerged. Burned and calcined matter indicated the probable destruction which had occurred.

When the excavations were completed, a fantastic city could be seen, finer by far than anything discovered previously.

According to legend, Proetus, the supposed King of Tiryns, had built his stronghold with the aid of seven Cyclopes. Heinrich, regarding the massive ruins, could

View of Tiryns.

well believe it might have been true. Some of the blocks
of stone used in the construction were as much as 6 feet
long by 3 feet wide, and 3 feet thick!

There was an outer wall protecting the homes of towns-
men, shops, warehouses, and stables. This wall was 15
feet thick. Then an inner enclosure surrounded the
king's palace. The walls here were 30 feet thick and almost 60 feet high.

The palace itself contained many pillared rooms.
Heinrich even found a bathroom where the heroes of
Homer had bathed and scented themselves, and oiled their
bodies before engaging in sports events or going off to
battle.

Heinrich found no treasure such as he had found at
Mycenae, but this citadel was more important than any
treasure. Once again Homer had been proved correct.
Once again a legend had been found to contain germs of
truth.

Heinrich pointed to the similarity of the vases he found
to those found at Mycenae, and by others in various places.
This must surely be proof that the whole area of the Greek
isles and parts of the mainland had contained a great
prehistoric civilization!

Heinrich was correct, but many years passed before the
picture was revealed, still more years before it was completely understood. But Heinrich pointed the way, and
others followed. He had dared, had risked the ridicule
—but triumphantly he was justified.

In his early sixties, Heinrich had yet another dream,
still more hope of proving his theory. He firmly believed

that the center of this complex civilization was to be found on the island of Crete.

"I should like," he said, "to crown my career with one great piece of work—the excavation of the prehistoric royal palace at Knossos, on Crete, which I believe I discovered three years ago."

Alas, it was not to be. He found himself in the same difficulties he had encountered so many years before at Troy. The governor of the island, who owned the site of Knossos, gave him permission to dig, but he wanted Heinrich to buy the land at the outrageous price of 100,-000 francs. Heinrich bargained with him until he had reduced that price to less than half. Part of the bargain was that Heinrich would own the 2,500 olive trees on the site. But when Heinrich counted the trees, he found fewer than nine hundred. He was still enough of a businessman to refuse to stand for such cheating and he was so angered by it that the whole agreement collapsed.

Heinrich gave a good deal of thought to a permanent home for the treasure of Troy. He knew he could not live forever, and, in fact, the pains in his ears and the dreadful headaches he suffered grew more frequent. He realized that the only places he had been treated kindly and taken seriously were America and England. He did not wish to offend either country. Yet the challenge to find acceptance from those who mocked him could not be denied. It was terribly hard to decide the right thing to do.

Then, one day, the answer came in a most unusual way. During one of his frequent excursions to ancient ruins,

Heinrich rested for a while at the foot of Mount Ida. Beside him was a man, a young scholar, who had become his friend and assistant, Rudolf Virchow. Virchow noticed that Heinrich seemed unusually depressed. He guessed what was worrying Heinrich for they had discussed the matter of a permanent home for the treasure often enough. He knew that Heinrich's depression at that moment was something more than another splitting headache.

Gazing at his old friend, Virchow suddenly reached out and plucked a sprig of blackthorn which he handed to Heinrich, saying: "A present from Ankershagen."

(Later, Virchow said that the words came to his lips unbidden.)

Heinrich was stunned. Memories of his childhood, the struggles of his life, flooded through his mind. Then his eyes lit up with relief and pleasure as he accepted the sprig of flowering thorn. Both men knew that the solution to the problem of the treasure had been found.

"Of course," Heinrich murmured. "It must go to Germany. I will leave all arrangements in your capable hands, Rudolf."

It took a long time for Virchow to get his proposals to the German Kaiser, but he finally succeeded. A period of feting followed, and Heinrich and Sophia were entertained by German royalty. Heinrich was given the Freedom of the City of Berlin, and awarded the Order of Merit. The treasure was placed in a museum in Berlin, the German capital.

There were many who begrudged Heinrich his

triumph.   With the royal family accepting his gifts in the name of Germany, Heinrich could afford to ignore them. But he found it hard to forgive those who had sneered at his accomplishments and those who had belittled him in the press.   But in this roundabout way, he silenced and defeated them.

One result of the furor aroused by Heinrich's work was that various sites of antiquity in Greece and Turkey were now swarming with archeologists and tourists.   Heinrich himself remained very active.   He divided his time between attending to his vast business interests and making expeditions into the past.   But he found no more treasures or anything of importance.   He was beginning to tire, but the frantic frog still hopped about the capitals of Europe.

But time was running out.   Several operations had failed to ease the pains in his ears, and his headaches were gruesome to endure.   His cold sea baths only aggravated the trouble.   Heinrich was growing old.

Under the prodding and persuading of Sophia and Rudolf Virchow, Heinrich decided to enter a clinic in Paris and try one more operation to ease his pain.   The doctors later assured him that the operation had been a complete success, but Heinrich felt no better.

Instinct still served Heinrich well, and he listened to its voice of warning.   He knew the end was near.   He telegraphed Sophia, who was anxiously awaiting news of him in Athens: "I am coming home.   Hold up Christmas until I arrive."

Heinrich felt too tired and ill to make the journey by

sea. Instead, he set out from Paris, traveling overland. On the way, he stopped for a while to admire the remains of Pompeii and spent some time browsing in the museums of Naples.

On Christmas Day, 1890, while walking across the *Piazza della Santa Carità,* Heinrich collapsed on the pavement. A crowd soon surrounded the little man. Wildly, Heinrich's eyes swept over the faces staring down upon him in his agony. The power of speech had deserted him! He was partially paralyzed.

The icy fingers of coldness reached out for Heinrich's heart for the last time. He felt more terribly lonely than ever before.

A policeman pushed aside the crowd. "What's going on here?" he demanded.

"The poor man just dropped to the pavement," a woman said. "He cannot move and he cannot speak."

Heinrich was perfectly conscious and his eyes bored into the face of the policeman in a desperate effort to communicate, but in vain. Heinrich was carried to a hospital. He was examined briefly and the policeman was told, "He's only had a fainting spell. We've no room for such cases here. You'll have to take him somewhere else."

The bewildered policeman did not know what else to do so he carried Heinrich to the police station. There, they searched Heinrich but found his pockets empty— except for a small slip of paper which, at first, they only glanced at. Giving it a closer look, a policeman said, "This is the name of a doctor. He lives nearby."

This slip of paper was all that stood between Heinrich

Schliemann, the millionaire archeologist, and oblivion in a pauper's grave.

Fortunately, the doctor was at home and came to the police station at once. There, he found Heinrich lying on the ground in the courtyard. He knelt down to examine him.

"Why do you take so much interest in this man?" a police sergeant asked. "Surely he is poor and cannot pay for your services? Who is he? And what are we to do with him?"

The doctor reached inside Heinrich's shirt. Holding up a bag of gold coins he held it before the startled eyes of the police. "As you can see," he said, "he is far from being a poor man. He is a very famous man and he pays me well. Help me get him back to his hotel."

While they made preparations to move him, the doctor leaned over Heinrich. "Can you understand me, Dr. Schliemann? If you can, nod your head." With relief in his eyes, Heinrich nodded his head. He was in very great pain.

"We are taking you to your hotel. I have summoned some of my colleagues. They will be waiting for us and we shall discuss what must be done. I will tell you the decision when I have consulted with them. Try not to worry. I shall notify your wife immediately."

Carefully, they placed Heinrich in his bed. He could hear the soft voices in the adjoining room. Alone, with not a soul to look upon, and no human being to witness his departure, Heinrich Schliemann died.

Early in January, Heinrich's body was taken home to

the grieving, heartbroken Sophia. Tenderly, Sophia put her husband to rest in the good earth, where lay buried so much of the world he had never known but which he had brought back from the dim past for all men to see, that they might know their origins. The blue Mediterranean sky that had looked down upon his ancient heroes now looked down upon Heinrich's resting place.

Many kings, nobles, scholars, and others who had denied Heinrich Schliemann the honor and acceptance he had so desired in his lifetime, now came forward to lay wreaths at his tomb and honor him in death.

In a shaky hand, a dying Gladstone in England wrote to the sorrowing Sophia:

His enthusiasm called back into being the ancient spirit of chivalry in a thoroughly pure and bloodless form. He had to encounter in the early stages of his work both frowns and indifference, yet the one and the other alike had to give way, as the force and value of his discoveries became clear, like mists upon the sun.

And the legend of the unlikely hero was born.

The Meaning and the Mystery

HEINRICH SCHLIEMANN died believing firmly that he had discovered and unearthed the Troy of King Priam. He was convinced of the authenticity of the golden mask of Agamemnon—but Heinrich made mistakes.

The mistakes he made, his errors of judgment, can be readily understood. If America suddenly ceased to exist —how perplexing it would be for some future archeologist to re-create its history! Treasures would be found— relics of cultures drawn from the four corners of the world—side by side with purely American objects and artifacts. Only an alert scholar, willing to use his imagination, to take chances and see a kinship between his own civilization and the one he was exploring, would find the answer. He would deduce accurately that America had been a great trading civilization with business all over the world. He would know that older oddities represented treasures that had been traded and brought to America by adventurous, traveling individuals. The answer to such puzzles usually lies in the mind of the beholder—as long as he remembers that human nature remains constant.

Sophia Schliemann was correct. History made its judgment and has been kind to Heinrich. When the ledgers were closed, the balance was seen to be heavily in favor of Heinrich. His mistakes were human, understandable. They resulted largely from overeagerness and the goading taunts of skeptics. But when his work was done, this strange man, from his hard life, had left the world wiser, a better place for his having lived in it. His detractors have mostly been lost in the limbo where all small minds belong.

It was left to Sir Arthur Evans, the boy who had sat enthralled so many years before, to give the proof of value Heinrich Schliemann so desperately sought. In his own great work, Sir Arthur Evans established beyond any shadow of doubt the truth of a widespread prehistoric civilization such as Heinrich believed in. Heinrich Schliemann had, indeed, unearthed the Troy of King Priam. What Henrich could not know was that he had gone back far before that, into the history of a civilization that had flourished more than 6,000 years B.C. He had failed to recognize the great stones he'd believed in as a boy—and dug beneath them.

The impetus Heinrich Schliemann gave to the science of archeology has built with ever-increasing momentum. The exact science as we know it today has grown from the boldness of action, the slow and painful development of methods foreshadowed by the work of Heinrich Schliemann. It would have pleased Heinrich very much to know that today he is often referred to as "the father of modern archeology." The world gasped at the magnifi-

cent picture Sir Arthur Evans revealed to it when he
paused to pay tribute to Heinrich:

I had the happiness to make his [Schliemann's] acqaintance
on the fields of his glory, and I still remember the echoes of
his visits to England, which were his greatest scenes of triumph.
Something of the romance of his earlier years still seemed to
cling to his personality, and I have myself an almost uncanny
memory of the spare, darkly clad, slightly built man, of sallow
complexion, wearing spectacles through which—so fancy took
me—he looked deep into the ground.

Evans did his greatest work uncovering the palace of
King Minos and establishing the truth of the mythical
Minoan civilization. This incredibly rich and beautiful
civilization was old when the ancient Greeks were loosely
knit tribes of barbarians. He had found the fountain-
head of our civilization. Although these proved to be the
"people of the lands of the sea" described by the ancient
Egyptians with whom they traded, the Minoan civilization was not Oriental but Western. The myths of
Daedalus and Icarus, of Theseus and the Minotaur, now
had their bases fixed firmly in fact. The strange treasures
found by Heinrich could not be placed in proper context.
They were different from classical Greek work and much
of their oddity stemmed from contact with Minos. The
Minoans were a great naval power and a great trading
people.

Without realizing it, Heinrich had gone beneath the
level of his Trojan heroes. Evans, when he examined
Heinrich's work, found the city many levels higher than
Heinrich had supposed. Heinrich had dug far into the

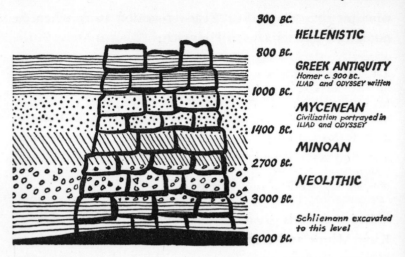

300 BC.

HELLENISTIC

800 BC.

GREEK ANTIQUITY
Homer c. 900 BC.
ILIAD and ODYSSEY written

1000 BC.

MYCENEAN
Civilization portrayed in
ILIAD and ODYSSEY

1400 BC.

MINOAN

2700 BC.

NEOLITHIC

3000 BC.

Schliemann excavated
to this level

6000 BC.

past, to the ancient world that gave birth to the world of
Priam and Agamemnon and the Trojan heroes.

It is largely accepted today that Homer's Troy is to
be found at the seventh level of the stratified excavations.
From all these deep roots has grown our own civilization.

And what of the future?

Sometimes together, sometimes separately, often over-
lapping, the sciences of geology and archeology are uncovering the story of man's past. New tools are coming
into the hands of scientists with bewildering rapidity.
With these tools at their command, geologists and archeologists will continue to go back into man's past—while
he struggles ahead to his future. Sooner or later, man
may discover a germ of truth for the nagging, persistent
legends of the lost continent of Atlantis. Perhaps he may
learn, through deep cores taken from the ocean bed,

whether or not some cataclysmic combination of earth-quake and glacier sank the mythical Atlantis beneath the waves of a tortured ocean.   Man may find a common denominator, some basis to point a common origin of the great pyramid structures scattered across a wide belt of the earth, with recurring symbols among peoples thought to have had no contact with one another.   Could these scattered symbols originate with the survivors of Atlantis?

When we see science, day after day, turn yesterday's "impossible" into today's commonplace—it is a bold man who will not admit . . . *it might be!*

Heinrich Schliemann's treasure of Troy rested in the museum of Berlin until World War II.   The bombers, which the Nazis said would never touch Berlin, dropped their murderous loads, night after night, then day after day, with sickening regularity.   All art treasures were removed to places of safety.

The treasures of Troy were buried deep in a bunker beneath the Berlin Zoo.   When the Russians entered the city in 1945, they found this treasure and carted it off to Russia.

The Russians issued a report in 1958, claiming that all such treasures were being returned to East Germany. At the present time, however, there is no knowledge that this has been done.

Perhaps, one day, the fabulous treasures of Troy will once again emerge from hiding, be brought from their second secret abode and exhibited and admired anew— as Heinrich Schliemann would devoutly wish them to be.

Bibliography

NOTE: For the dialogue employed in this book, the author has relied upon his own imagination, but Heinrich Schliemann left us many valuable records of his life and his work in archeology which are a rich source of information for the student and scholar.

It is the author's hope that he has passed along to his reader some of the inspiration he discovered in the following fine books and articles, most of which are readily available to the reader and all of which were helpful in the preparation of *The Unlikely Hero*.

Blind, Karl, "The great pathfinder in Trojan and pre-Hellenic antiquity." *Asiatic Quarterly Review:* Woking, 1892.

Ceram, C. W., *Gods, Graves & Scholars, The Story of Archaeology*. New York: Alfred A. Knopf, 1954.

Cottrell, Leonard, *The Bull of Minos*. New York: Rinehart & Company, Inc., 1958.

Durant, Will, *The Life of Greece, The Story of Civilization*. New York: Simon & Schuster, Inc., 1939.

Guinagh, Kevin, *Inspired Amateurs*. London, New York: Longmans, Green & Company, 1937.

Lavalette, Vigée, "Heinrich Schliemann." *Modern Mystic*, London: 1938, vol. 2, pp. 92–96.

Ludwig, Emil, *Schliemann, The Story of a Gold Seeker*. Boston: Little, Brown & Company, 1931.

"Man Who Found Troy." *Atlantic Monthly* 188: 61–66, November, 1951.

Melas, A. S., "Most Unforgettable Character I've Met." *Reader's Digest* 56: 73–78, June, 1950.

"Old Worlds to Conquer." *Time* 58: 120, November 12, 1951.

Payne, Robert, *The Gold of Troy*. New York: Funk & Wagnalls Company, 1958.

Renault, Mary, *The King Must Die*. New York: Pantheon Books, Inc., 1958.

Schliemann, Heinrich, *Schliemann's First Visit to America, 1850–1851;* edited by Shirley H. Weber. Published for the American School of Classical Studies at Athens, Harvard University Press, 1942.

Ilios. The city and country of the Trojans. The results of researches and discoveries on the sites of Troy and throughout the Troad in the years

1871–72–73–78–79, including an autobiography of the author, by Dr. Heinrich Schliemann. With a preface, appendices, and notes by Professors Rudolf Virchow, Friedrich Max Müller, A. H. Sayce, J. P. Mahaffy, H. Brugsch-Bey, P. Ascherson, M. A. Postolaccas, M. E. Burnoff, Mr. Calvert, and Mr. A. J. Duffield. New York: Harper & Brothers [1880]

Mycenae. A narrative of researches and discoveries at Mycenae and Tiryns with preface by W. E. Gladstone. New York: Scribner, Armstrong & Co., 1878; new edition 1880.

Tiryns. The prehistoric palace of the Kings of Tiryns, the results of the latest excavations: by Dr. Henry Schleimann with preface by Professor F. Adler and contributions by Dr. Wm. Dorpfeld. New York: C. Scribner & Sons, 1885.

Troja. Results of the latest researches and discoveries on the site of Homer's Troy and in the heroic tumuli and other sites, made in the year 1882. And a narrative of a journey in the Troad in 1881. By Dr. Henry Schliemann with preface by Professor A. H. Sayce. New York: Harper & Brothers, 1884.

Troy and Its Remains; a narrative of researches and discoveries made on the site of Ilium, and in the Trojan plain. Tr. with the author's sanction. Ed. by Philip Smith. London: J. Murray, 1875.

Schurchardt, Karl, *Schliemann's Excavations: An archaeological and historical study.* Translated from the German by Eugenie Sellers. With an appendix, on the recent discoveries at Hissarlik by Dr. Schliemann and Dr. Dorpfeld. London: Macmillan & Co., Ltd., 1891.

Turner, G. A., "Odyssey of Heinrich Schliemann." *il Design* 53: 142–43 March, 1952.

Index

About the Author and Artist

ALAN HONOUR is, in his own words, "American by choice, British by birth." He was born in London in 1918 and remained there to study until 1939, when he joined the Royal Air Force. Radio Intelligence assigned him first to Norway, then to France, and finally to the Middle East for four years.

After the war, Mr. Honour returned to London. From there he went to France and to Italy, where he worked on film scripts. After that stint he traveled on to the United States, which is now his home. He lives in Richmond, Indiana.

In addition to *The Unlikely Hero,* he is the author of *Ten Miles High, Two Miles Deep: The Adventures of the Piccards,* and *Cave of Riches: The Story of the Dead Sea Scrolls.*

GRISHA DOTZENKO, who is known to the art world by his professional name, Grisha, was born in the Ukraine in 1925. He attended art school in Moscow but left the country to fight with the Allies during World War II. Grisha came to the United States in 1947 and has since become an American citizen. He attended the Art Students League and is now planning his own art show of painting, sculpture and woodcuts for the spring of 1960. His artwork has appeared in many other junior books, including the series on Africa by John Gunther, published by Harper and Brothers. The artist now lives in New York with his family.